Improving Education
in a World of Politics

Other Books by M. Scott Norton

The Principal as a Learning-Leader:
Motivating Students by Emphasizing Achievement

Competency-Based Leadership:
A Guide for High Performance in the Role of the School Principal

Teachers with the Magic:
Great Teachers Change Students' Lives

The Changing Landscape of School Leadership:
Recalibrating the School Principalship

The Legal World of the School Principal:
What Leaders Need to Know about School Law

Guiding Curriculum Development:
The Need to Return to Local Control

Guiding the Human Resources Function in Education:
New Issues, New Needs

A Guide for Educational Policy Governance:
Effective Leadership for Policy Development

Dealing with Change:
The Effects of Organizational Development on Contemporary Practices

The White House and Education through the Years:
U.S. Presidents' Views and Significant Education Contributions

Improving Education in a World of Politics

Recommendations and Strategies for Effective Political Participation

M. Scott Norton

ROWMAN & LITTLEFIELD
Lanham • Boulder • New York • London

Published by Rowman & Littlefield
An imprint of The Rowman & Littlefield Publishing Group, Inc.
4501 Forbes Boulevard, Suite 200, Lanham, Maryland 20706
www.rowman.com

Unit A, Whitacre Mews, 26–34 Stannary Street, London SE11 4AB

British Library Cataloguing in Publication Information Available

Library of Congress Cataloging-in-Publication Data Available

ISBN: 978-1-4758-4312-5 (cloth alk. paper)
ISBN: 978-1-4758-4313-2 (pbk. alk. paper)
ISBN: 978-1-4758-4314-9 (electronic)

∞™ The paper used in this publication meets the minimum requirements of American National Standard for Information Sciences—Permanence of Paper for Printed Library Materials, ANSI/NISO Z39.48–1992.

Printed in the United States of America

Contents

Politics Preface

WHY THE BOOK WAS WRITTEN

The primary focus of the book is to underscore the fact that education is directly influenced by the ongoing politics of the social, economic, legal, and legislative decisions that take place within the internal and external environments in which it exists. Increasingly, the problems and issues facing the states and the nation have found their way to the doorsteps of local school boards, school superintendents' offices, school principals' offices, and teachers' classrooms. It is clear that the greater the diversity of political action surrounding an educational issue or problem the more probable is the continuance of high-pressure political involvement at the local school level.

School leaders have contended that they are not adequately prepared to participate in the political matters facing them in their administrative roles. Few administrator preparation programs place emphasis on the topic of politics and education. Power structure analysis is foreign to the large majority of school leaders. As one school principal stated, "I have always done my best to avoid getting involved in the 'dirty world' of politics. In fact, my superiors have cautioned me about doing so." Although most administrator preparation programs spend considerable time on the topic of decision-making, common internal and external influences present in the making of important decisions are largely overlooked.

The book emphasizes the need for school leaders to become better prepared in the areas of power structure analysis and the identification of the power persons within the community who have strong influence on what decisions will be approved or not approved. The book contends that just reacting to change mandates and proposed school policies will continue to occur unless school leaders become effective participants in education's world of politics. Without such involvement, local control will continue to decrease. New strategies in administrative management must include specific attention to power structure analysis in a position of leadership as opposed to followership. Empirical evidence suggests that school personnel spend the majority of their time talking to themselves. However, research studies have revealed that the citizenry has concluded that educators operate in a closed system. In fact, school-level principals, who know most about the education problems and issues being faced, report that they are unable to address the school publics. That is, the school district's central office spokesperson is the one authorized to speak publicly for the schools. The book's content is opposed to this position.

Effective involvement in the politics of education requires effective preparation for doing so, and a new policy for educator involvement in the political world is a requirement for all school leaders. As stated in the opening paragraph of this preface, many different persons and groups are increasingly being involved in political issues related to education. However, all too often the conflicts are among educators themselves. Teachers vs. administrators, teachers vs. the school board, parents versus the school leaders, students versus the school administrators, and students versus the state governance bodies. Student walkouts and sit-ins are increasing in number. Teacher strikes are increasing, and school boards are losing their local control. The book sets forth cooperative strategies and guidelines whereby educators and their clients can increase their effectiveness in working together politically for the betterment of educational purposes and practices.

Introduction

HOW THE BOOK IS ORGANIZED

The contents of the book center on: (1) politics of education with a backward glance and a look to the future. Chapter 1 underscores the fact that education is directly influenced by the ongoing politics of the social, economic, and legislative decisions that take place in the internal and external environments in which it functions; (2) chapter 2 focuses on the many factors that influence the policies and practices of local school districts. Various boards/agencies, governments, organizations, associations, and other groups are recommending, mandating, participating, and legislating ways and means for local schools to program the learning content for student learning; (3) chapter 3 centers on school-community power structures and how these influential individuals and groups go about influencing the decision-making process of the local schools; and (4) chapter 4 provides guidelines for the local school leaders to increase their knowledge and skills in the political world in which they operate.

School board members, school superintendents, school principals, and other practicing education leaders will find the book of special value. The content of the chapters points out clearly that the environment of educational programs and practices will be decided increasingly in a political context. Either educational personnel must wake to the need for them to participate effectively in policy development process or the loss of local control will continue to be patronized. Political knowledge and skill can be improved, but administrator programs must redefine their programs to include courses and field experiences in politics, and other members of education must be involved in ongoing development programs that center on such topics as power structure analysis, local school district policy development, and open school communication strategies in which all school personnel are effective in participating.

Each chapter opens with a statement of primary purpose. A summary of key ideas and recommendations is set forth at the close of each chapter. The book's glossary contains many terms that are found commonly in the social, economic, and legislative world of contemporary politics. Discussion questions are provided at the end of each chapter for extended learning purposes. In addition, case studies are set forth at the close of each chapter. Brief quizzes are used in some chapters for the purpose of engaging the reader additionally into the objectives of the chapter.

Chapter 1

Politics of Education:
A Backward Glance and
a Look to the Future

Primary Chapter Goal: To underscore the fact that education is directly influenced by the ongoing politics of the social, economic, and legislative decisions that take place in the internal and external environments in which it functions.

Throughout history, groups and individuals have been interested in the question "Who has the ear of the King?" Today, we continue to be interested in the politics and power influences that result in decisions as to how the nation's values and resources are allocated over a period of time. How decisions about educational issues are determined and who makes these decisions are central to what we refer to generally as *the politics of education*.

Few if any of the social, economic, and legislative education decisions have total consensus; most are surrounded with controversy and vested interests. Many educational issues and their related problems, previously resolved at the local school level, have become state responsibilities and national concerns. It is clear that the greater the diversity of political action surrounding an educational issue/problem, the less probable will be the continuation of low-pressure involvement. Few persons will argue today that education must be kept out of politics.

As Root (1998, May 1) has noted, "The principal ground of reproach against any American citizen should be that he is not a politician. Everyone ought to be, as Lincoln was" (p. 1). Root noted further that politics are the practical exercise of self-government, and somebody must attend to it if we are to have self-government. Thus, it is imperative that educators and others interested in the status of education nationally be intelligently involved in its political issues and related problems.

Nolan Estes, former school superintendent and professor of educational administration at the University of Texas, presented his ideas on education's

1

involvement in politics in a speech to University Council of Educational Administration members. He noted that no reference that he had ever consulted said, "Let's keep politics out of education and education out of politics." He had a hunch that it was Thomas De Quincey, the man who wrote *Confessions of an Opium Eater*. He must have hatched this line one evening while he was viewing Utopia through a narcotic haze for it reflects neither reality nor sobriety. He went on to say that "perhaps in some Utopia of the future, politics will play no part in education. But as long as we have public schools and as long as public funds support the education of our young, politics will affect, in a major way, school policies and practices."

The chapter objective is to summarize the realities of political influence that have pervaded the education policy-making procedures in the United States. This approach is not that of perspectives and outcomes of national presidential administrations, but those more direct and influential factors that have invaded local policy decisions in education and have served to change the administration in such ways as mandating curricular program provisions and instructional procedures for implementing them.

EDUCATIONAL CHANGES
AND POLITICS OF EDUCATION

Just about every group in the nation has something to say about improving the quality of education. At one point in history, one publication reported that some 275 special commissions, task forces, and committees were focusing on education reforms. Recommendations for reform have been far reaching and have included calls for major restructuring of America's public schools. Charter schools represent only one form of restructuring. Federal government intervention into virtually every component of state and local school governance has increased significantly.

In the late 1950s, the stir for relevancy focused on a renewal of mathematics, science, and foreign language programs in schools. Federal intervention in matters of education increased rapidly with such events as *Sputnik* and the 1983 publication, *A Nation at Risk*, that served to underscore the problems of the fading quality of education in America and pointed out the lack of educational standards that was wreaking havoc with the nation's ability to compete in the international market.

In the early 1960s, James Conant Bryant popularized the term "educational establishment" suggesting that education was a *closed system* with only a few individuals in the *inner circles* deciding the policy issues. As one writer reportedly said, not all solutions rest in better organization of a closed system. Education was being viewed as becoming less and less relevant to the interests and needs of society.

CHANGES IN INVOLVEMENT
AND CONTROL OF THE PUBLIC SCHOOLS

School boards and school personnel are facing ongoing changes that directly influence their ability to govern the school district's programs. Some of the entries in the following listing have been in place for several years, others are more contemporary, and others would be considered as ongoing.

A. Taxpayers and Financial Reform

   1. Ways in which school funds are distributed
   2. The pressures for states to assume more responsibility for financing education
   3. The setting of tax ceilings for funding school costs
   4. The loss of local control of taxation and bonding authority

B. Students and Their Rights

   1. Change regarding the citizen rights of students in relation to free speech, dress, privacy, and human rights
   2. Due process rights to assure fair treatment

C. Teachers Rights and Organizational Power

   1. Participate in management expectations
   2. Ongoing pressures for empowerment
   3. Professional negotiation rights
   4. Political influence of teacher unions
   5. Continuous struggle for increasing teachers' salaries with corresponding teacher turnover

D. Federal and State Controls through Mandates and Legislation

   1. External mandates related to teacher evaluations, curriculum requirements, teaching methods, accountability, and testing requirements
   2. Legislation and mandates that reduce local school controls
   3. Ongoing accountability in relation to student achievement
   4. Mandated state and federal requirements that are not accompanied by adequate funding
   5. Lack of adequate financial support by state and federal sources

E. Increase in Various Pressure Groups and Vested-Interest Community Power Individuals

   1. Increase in educational controls of budgets and programs by state governors
   2. Power authorities who favor the charter school program and related private and parochial school programs

F. Other Political Forces Affecting the Local School's Ability to Survive

1. The increasing number of vested-interest groups
2. Social impacts on what the school is to do and not to do
3. Recommendations from conflicting sources on such matters as teacher pay, school curriculum, and school rules
4. Problems that must be faced and resolved such as teacher retention, teacher load, bullying, student discipline procedures, achievement expectations, student violence, drug abuse, social media, and related student dropout problems

CITIZEN PARTICIPATION IN EDUCATIONAL MATTERS AND RESULTING ACCOUNTABILITY

Although no group wants to accept fault for education's ills, it seems that the lineup for receiving credit for recommended solutions is rather crowded. Politically, government agencies, study groups, educators themselves, and a variety of other individuals and groups have set forth actions designed to make schools more effective and relevant. School leaders themselves have encouraged more involvement in school activities on the part of their constituents. This belief seemed to suggest that if the school's publics knew more about educational practices they would learn to understand and support what the schools were doing right.

The public took seriously education's plea to get involved. Yet, the more that the citizenry became involved in school matters, the more often they complained about the closed system of their schools. In the past, such groups as the parent-teacher association and other citizen advisory groups have provided arenas for building consensus and simplifying the school board's decision-making tasks. Increased public participation resulted in various forms of shared control such as: (1) different clientele running for school board positions; (2) site-based representative councils at local schools that were implemented to give a direct voice of teachers, parents, and students in the program decisions of the school; and (3) specific ways for local school-community members to provide recommendations for the local school principal and the school district's school board to consider for the betterment of school program procedures.

The behavior of local school principals and other school administrators was influenced greatly by this new participation. Parents and other citizens not only asked good questions about school budgets and other policy matters, but they also focused on what was being offered in the school's instructional programs. These involvements led to further challenges by parents and other members of the school community, concerning the quality of outcomes in relation to student achievement. "Get tough" approaches were evidenced throughout education as well as pushes for reforms in teacher education and in the preparation programs for educational administrators.

By the mid-1980s, many states had adopted new requirements in the areas of teacher proficiency. The National Policy Board was established in 1989 for the primary purpose of improving preparation programs for school administrators. For example, one of the board's recommendations called for the requirement of the doctoral degree for all administrators in charge of a school or school system. History has shown that such a recommendation was not to be implemented. Just retaining individuals in the challenging role of the school principalship was problematic enough.

A LOOK AT PARTICIPATIVE RESULTS

Former views of parent-teacher associations as being important for helping schools to purchase stage curtains or other school supplies were changed toward political agenda that challenged the singular authority of school professionals. Some professional groups, such as the University Council for Educational Administration (UCEA), contested the quality of those persons who were entering public school administration. By the 1990s, educational decision-making and public participation were virtually synonymous.

The tenure terms of school superintendents and principals have waned. While the past often witnessed public school superintendents practicing in a specific school district for fifteen to twenty years, the average term for one superintendency today commonly is five to six years. For school principals, some reports state that school principalships turns over every two to three years on the average. In the 1980s, for example, Chicago, Cleveland, Boston, Seattle, and Denver each had three school superintendents in less than five years. Such results led to an increase of investigations relative to the type of power structures that existed in various school communities.

STUDYING POWER: POWER DEFINED

The earliest definition of *power* available to us was stated by Hobbes (1651) and reported in chapter 10 of his book titled *Leviathan* and later published by Penguin Books in 1981. Hobbes stated that power was a man's present means, to obtain some future apparent good. Many other definitions of *power* do exist, although the definitions tend to be quite similar. For example, Domhoff (2005) stated, "Power is about being able to realize wishes, to produce the effects you want to produce" (p. 1). Herrity (2010) stated that in its simplest form "power is the ability to exercise control or influence over another person or organization" (p. 1). Herrity serves to simplify the concept of community power structures by stating that there are only two types of gender power structures, although he points out that there are many other power bases that do exist in local communities. The one strategy for an individual, such as a school superintendent or school principal, is to recognize who are the *power influentials* in their community and to identify the sources of their power base.

Every school community has individuals who can provide information and support that adds to the possibility of making positive changes in school operations. These influentials are commonly persons who are knowledgeable of community culture and the needs of the community. Their voice can weigh heavily on policy decisions and program practices. Not all such influentials are officials in city government. They can be individuals who have received high respect on the part of community members for their active participation in community projects and their contributions to the overall welfare of the community.

Influentials can be of service to education in a variety of ways. First of all, these persons are well connected to community issues and much aware of the citizen's views on the various matters that occur in school communities everywhere. Their involvement in the issues facing school districts can be helpful since their association with the project gives credibility to it. The knowledge of influentials is of paramount importance in directing school leaders to other persons in the community that can give "best" advice as to actions to take and additional persons to include in the matter at hand. In addition, these respected persons often are able to suggest strategies for dealing effectively with individuals or groups that are likely to oppose the initiative that is being addressed.

The recommended ways to initiate communication with community influentials are set forth later in the chapter. We do note at this point that it is essential that plans for making direct contact with influential persons are of major importance. A school superintendent or school board president, for example, has implied power in view of the important positions that they hold. It would be uncommon for any other person in the school community to refuse a call or interview with one of these educational leaders. Personal communication comes high on the list of necessities when it comes to identifying persons in the know and gaining their views on matters of major importance facing the school district. It is recommended that school leaders seek the aid of a known community leader when contacting an influential that is unknown to them. In any case, personal contact is of paramount importance.

Figure 1.1 is an example pyramid of power influences that commonly exist within a local school environment. Although the figure is only illustrative,

Power influentials often behind the scenes
The Colonels
High-level influentials on policies and issues
The Captains
Local influentials in positions of big businesses and sometimes media leaders
The Lieutenants
Active local persons on school boards and chambers of commerce and city councils
The Sergeants
Active local persons who serve as officers of civic clubs and managers of big businesses
The Enlisted Employees
Administrators of the school district and often officers of the PTA, teacher and religious groups
The Supporting Teacher and Parent Groups
Interested parents, active students, and other school-community participants

Figure 1.1.   An Illustration: Local School-Community Power Structure

types of power do differ and the figure is presented as being an example rather than specific in regard to the structure of power that exists in all schools.

WHY GO TO ALL THIS TROUBLE?

Herrity (2010) lists several reasons as to why it is important for individuals such as school leaders to know and understand the nature of the community power structure: (1) gives official sanction (support) for official actions; (2) provides useful suggestions for implementing desirable projects and programs; (3) provides additional resources that serve to support desirable projects and programs that might otherwise not be available to you and/ or other community members; and (4) can give validation of the project or program to other members of the community.

Petress (2015, December 18) defines the term power as "the ability to influence others to believe, behave, or to value as those in power desire them to or to strengthen, validate, or confirm present beliefs, behaviors, or values" (p. 1). Petress goes on to say that power is a social force that allows select person to mobilize others, to organize others to act in concert; and to melt away resistance to leader's authority. In its simplest form, power is defined as the possibility to influence others.

Investigations tend to reach interesting conclusions about the type of power structures that exist in relation to the behavior and survival of the school superintendent and school board members. Do different types of community influentials, for example, dominate the decision-making outcomes of the school district? An early study by Hunter (1953), *Community Power Structure*, led the way for many follow-up studies on the topic of community power structures. Other such studies by Dahl (1958) and McCarty and Ramsey (1968) followed. McCarty's and Ramsey's study identified four primary power groups within school communities, elite, factional, pluralistic, and inert.

In the elite power structure, only 1 percent to 2 percent of the population was found to dominate the decision-making surrounding important policy decisions. Such dominance was viewed as being absolute. Studies of power structure suggested that the type of power structure of the community also was reflected in the local board of education. That is, if elite, one board member tends to dominate policy decisions. The school superintendent tends to "fit" the power structure represented. For example, in an elite power structure, the superintendent acts mainly as a functionary in carrying out board mandates. Whereas in a *factional power structure*, the superintendent must be much more of an arbitrator (see table 1.1).

The topic of community power structure is discussed throughout the chapters of the book. We must keep in mind that early studies of power structure, in the main, were administered when the diversity of citizenry in school districts was commonly quite different from those of today. Multicultural populations are more common today and tend to result in fewer communities being "dominated" by ruling elites in formerly white-dominated populations.

In addition, some persons today speak of the "Trump Effect" whereby the political climate has influenced the attitudes and behaviors of children, youth, and adults. A recent article by Richmond (2017, August 7) stated that some researchers have teamed up to study the "Trump Effect" on Canadian and American school communities. As stated by Richmond, "Schools are feeling

Table 1.1.   The Four Types of Power Structures and Corresponding Roles of the School Board and School Superintendent

Community Power Structure	School Board Role	School Superintendent's Function
Elite	Dominated	Functionary
Factional	Divided @ issue at hand	Political strategist
Pluralistic	Diverse	Professional advisor
Inert	Sanctionary	Decision-maker

reverberations of the political climate across border, and some educators are adjusting their lesson plans accordingly" (p. 1).

POLITICAL INFLUENCE SHOWS ITS PRESENCE IN MANY DIFFERENT ARENAS

The calls for more involvement in and control of schools have not been restricted to parents. The taxpayers generally have placed political pressures in such forms as: (1) pressing states to assume more responsibility for financing education; (2) the setting of tax ceilings for funding school costs and placing the decision of overriding the ceiling on the citizens/taxpayer themselves; (3) the ways school funds are distributed; and (4) placing more control of educational matters, above and beyond financial support, on the state. Thus, local control of education has become more troublesome. This is not to criticize the states' legal responsibility for education; rather legislative controls have tended to result in administrative controls in areas of curricular provisions and instructional methodology.

Those individuals and groups, who were backing school reform in the early 1970s, were finding that educational reform was extremely expensive. Those backing spending limits were in direct opposition of additional taxes. Even though the concern for improved education remained in the forefront, cost factors caused politicians and others to "back away" from education as their number-one concern. Quality and reform were found to be of such cost that "new taxes" were an obvious need. New taxes were not an attractive pursuit politically. In the 1970s, President Nixon expressed the view that just putting more money into education was not the answer for educational improvement.

STUDENTS AND THEIR RIGHTS

Within the walls of the schools, changes of political import have taken place. Formerly, students were in the position of being non-entities in the whole affair of governance in schools. The matter of how students were to dress, walk, speak, and act was generally prescribed in a unilateral way by school authorities. Now, students have gained specific rights of citizenship including due process and fair treatment. In the historic *Tinker vs. The Des Moines School District* case, the court ruled that even students had a right of freedom of speech when a basic constitutional right was being violated. When such rights were being exercised and did not interfere with school purposes or did not disrupt the learning of others, punishment was not in order. Due process and equal protection under the law became the byword for students and all citizens.

As a result, lists of student rights, including participative involvement in educational matters concerning student welfare, were drafted in schools nationally. School authority, as related to student "punishment," changed significantly. The procedures for dealing fairly with student behavior were in place. Unilateral administrative handling of student matters was no longer tolerated and certainly not politically astute. Even though the courts have reinstated certain authorities of school officials, such as locker searches, censorship, dress and speech, the due process rights of students added new dimensions to the once-unchallenged policy authority of the school. Due process proceedings through required hearings in relation to student suspension are typical in school activities today.

Student involvement in school political matters has been more patronizing than serious in nature. Student councils, representation on certain school committees, and rights relative to free speech and due process represent positive policy developments. Students have their own ideas on most every school matter that influences their learning opportunities. School personnel and others are wise to seek such involvement. Changes in student politics are revealed by such news headlines as "Teachers, Students Push for Change," "Students 'Walkout' to Demonstrate Need for Gun Control," and "Students Protest Outside Governor's Office for Education Support."

A Lightbulb Experience or the Heck They Are Not!

Times were tough in the Viewpoint Public School District. Budgets for school resources were to be reduced for the year by one-third, administrators' and teachers' salaries were frozen, and staff personnel were cut by 25 percent. The school board asked Superintendent Jenkins to have school principals meet with their teachers and with the site-based councils to discuss program reductions and resource alternatives. That is, could fees for certain student activities be increased to help cover fund reductions?

On this occasion, Principal Woods was to meet with the school's site-based council. The council consisted of four parents, two students, one staff member, three teachers and the school principal. Principal Woods opened the meeting thanking each member of the council for their services and, in this case, dealing with the school's major current problem, the lack of funds.

"I do not believe that increasing and adding student fees for our current program offerings is a good place to start," stated Principal Woods. "Our student activity fees are already resulting in parental complaints and loss of participation in some activities such as football, basketball and track. With the large monetary cuts facing us, there is little question that we'll have to look at program offerings, increases in class sizes, and the cutting of some of our extra-curricular offerings."

"We most likely will have to look at some of our common curricular classes and after-school activities," said assistant principal, Melanie Miller. "For one thing, the proposed swimming and volley ball programs will have to be on hold," she went on to say.

Mr. Kelly, a council member and local bank president, asked for the floor. "We are not spending money on swimming or volley ball now, so that won't save us any money," he commented. "After all, I've never believed that schools ought to be spending taxpayers' money on entertainment, schools are supposed to be focused on learning, citizenship, and the development of the characteristics that enable students to live and participate effectively as a citizen in a democracy."

"May I respond to Mr. Kelly?," asked Delmar Frederickson, a school senior and president of the senior class.

"Certainly," responded Principal Woods.

"If we were to list ten programs or subjects that could be cut, football and the other sports of basketball, track, and baseball would not even be on my list," said Delmar. "Yes, I agree, students are in school to learn, but participation in such activities as sports provides many positive opportunities to learn and build one's character. Please let me mention a few of them. First, sports like football require teamwork that is most important in any future work activities. The importance of health and physical conditioning is most important as well. The characteristics of leadership and responsibility are developed in any sport that a student chooses to participate. The significance of preparation looms most important in being a successful team. A player learns to appreciate winning but also learns what needs to be done after losing which is a character builder. Sportsmanship, competition, leadership, strategy, and responsibility loom important as well."

Delmar went on to say, "Last year in our class on math applications, Mrs. Kilpatrick took the entire class down to the gymnasium and divided the class into six groups of four students. Each group had to find answers to the following questions: (1) What is the square footage of the basketball court? Our school band has 52 members and each band member needs one square yard of space, would all the members be able to stand on the basketball court? (2) What is the circumference of the basketball hoop? What is the circumference of a basketball? Could two basketballs be placed across the diameter of the hoop? (3) How long is a three-point shot? (4) What are the dimensions of the basketball court, its length and width? How many square feet is that? How many square yards? (4) A football field's playing length is 100 yards and its width is 160 feet or 53.3 yards. How many basketball courts can be placed on a football field? Our next math lesson centered on metric measurements. We received extra credit for answering all of the foregoing questions in metrics. In addition—"

"Ok, Ok!" said board member Kelly, "You've helped me see the light. Let's not give up on adding swimming and volleyball after all."

INCREASING STUDENT POLITICS: STUDENT WALKOUTS AND SIT-INS

At the time of this writing, thousands of students throughout the nation were marching in protests relating to gun violence. The protests were part of National Walkout Day calling for an end to gun violence in America. The shootings in a Florida high school in February 2018, that resulted in the deaths of 17 victims was the primary tragedy that prompted the nation's students to take their political actions. Reportedly, more than 2,800 schools and colleges nationally participated in the walkout activities.

Students demonstrated on their own school grounds, at state capitols, in mayor's offices and during state legislative sessions. In one state's legislative session, a moment of silence was taken in honor of the deaths of the seventeen students in Florida. At the end of the silence, students in the galley yelled, "Never again," and walked out.

STUDENT POLITICAL ACTIVITIES AT THE UNIVERSITY LEVEL: A FORCE OF SIGNIFICANCE

Student involvement in political activities has been witnessed by virtually every university in America. Student political activity has become so common in higher education that universities nationally have adopted governance policies that tend to encourage student participation and promote discussion on political and civic issues and involvement in political affairs. A prime example of such action is exemplified by the policy actions of Xavier University in Cincinnati, Ohio. Xavier University's student lobbying, Political and Campaign Activities Policy for students encourages student involvement in political issues but does state that students should check with the Office of Student Involvement to ensure that the student activities fall within the university's policies and guidelines (Xavier University, 2016).

Eight specific areas of student political involvement are set forth in Xavier's policy statement: (1) candidate appearances, forums, and debates; (2) candidate endorsement and campaigning; (3) financial support; (4) use of university facilities; (5) use of university resources; (6) voter education; (7)

voter registration; and (8) voter transportation. The approval process, appeals process, violations of policy, policy review and amendment procedures, and contact procedures are detailed as well. The openness of the university's policy is a positive feature but does demonstrate a controlled procedure for student political activities with an appeals process for any denial of an activity that is requested but denied.

Each of the foregoing policy topics is explained in the policy statement. For example, entry number 1, candidate appearances, forums, and debates, sets forth three guidelines for its implementation. In brief, recognized student organizations may receive permission to provide speaking opportunities to public officials and/or candidates for public office. The appearance of a public official or candidate should be for an educational or information talk to the university community and must be sponsored by a recognized student organization. The procedures go on to say just how arrangements for such political activities should be communicated with the Director of Government Relations.

TEACHERS' RIGHTS AND POLITICAL EMPOWERMENT

The human relations movement that blossomed in the early 1920s gave major force to the concept of personnel involvement in policy development, including the involvement of teacher personnel. This early movement, led by such individuals as Mary Parker Follett, Elton Mayo, Kurt Lewin, Frederick Herzberg, Douglas McGregor, Abraham Maslow, and others, centered on the importance of positive human treatment in organizations and the ways in which people could contribute to the organization's purposes.

The era with its emphasis on internal democracy served as a major force in bringing about teacher participation in the decision-making process. A key term in school politics ultimately evolved as *empowerment* that now applies to all groups who seek a greater voice in school matters. *Site-based management, decentralization, collaboration*, and *participative management* also serve to describe the push of teachers' groups to gain more power in policy decisions in all matters of school operations.

The foregoing notion of teachers' rights was accepted generally until the 1960s. Strong opposition to teacher involvement in school activities, such as salaries, budgeting, tenure, workload, and other administrative matters, received strong administrative opposition. The procedure of *employee/professional negotiations* resulted in serious divisions among teacher and administrative personnel in school districts nationally. Impasse in negotiation practices led to the increase of teacher strikes. Teacher and administrator cooperation and collaboration were troublesome indeed.

Teachers have exercised their political clout in various ways. Their expertise as negotiators and lobbyists is one example. It was reported by Wirt and Kirst (1982) that there were only 35 teacher strikes between 1955 and 1965. But during 1967 and 1968 there were 114 strikes and another 131 strikes the following year. By 1985, the political threat of a teachers' strike was as much a part of the fall scene as the opening of the football season.

During the years that followed, although serious teacher strikes tended to lessen, the one-time philosophy that schools should be apolitical has evaporated. Political activities that are designed to influence policy decisions and gain advantages for one group or another are among the priorities of educational groups today. Teacher associations, state and national, have been directly involved in all matters of public education. Their numbers alone were important in political decisions. According to one report, by the mid-1970s, the nation's teachers were moving closer and closer to the number of farmers in the United States, and their numbers substantially outnumbered teamsters, auto-workers, steel workers, and physicians.

Over time, the "estimated" number of teachers in the United States rose to 5 million. A separate report stated that there were 751,000 farmers or ranchers in the United States. Although interesting from a political influence point of view, it is difficult at best to obtain substantial accuracy on such statistics. For example, how many different kinds of farmers exist in the nation? And which farmers might be included in any statistical report? The point, however, is that today teachers' numbers alone hold high potential for influence in educational policy decisions.

Although it can be argued that the political agenda by teachers has led to advantages for them, it is now well known that the aura of teachers being apolitical is a myth and thus education and teachers' groups find themselves in competition with other groups which seek the tax dollar for their own vested interests. Thus, in the arena where the allocation of dollars is determined, teachers' groups have become just another of the political pressure groups that seek favor above others in their claims for dollars. At the time of this writing, school teachers in Virginia had been on strike for several weeks and teachers in Arizona also were on the verge of doing the same.

In any case, the factor of teacher organizations has reflected in a new force with which school authorities and other decision-makers must deal. In addition, teacher groups themselves are now involved in efforts to respond to other political groups and view their own agendas as having first priority, and open conflict has become more in evidence. Thus, the struggle for political control of education within the states continues. The intervention of federal and state authorities has weighed heavily on the financial support for public education.

FEDERAL AND STATE AUTHORITY

Among the listing of major problems of school administrators and school boards in the United States has been that of the intervention/mandates by governments and other legal bodies. In the minds of many school publics is the belief that local authorities have constituted major road blocks to needed school reform. Various groups have secured state/federal legislation or court rulings that have intervened in the matters of control and administration of local school authority. These actions, of course, have impinged on local school authority and inhibited the ability to keep local control at hand. As we have learned, the closer that policy-making moves to the central agencies of government, the more blurred becomes the line of demarcation between educational politics and other forms of politics.

Each of the state and federal agencies of government has generated many new demands on schools. The demands come in various forms, including legislative mandates, court rulings, reporting requirements, testing, monitoring, and evaluating. Each of these demands places certain restraints on school personnel and indeed constitutes new work requirements on school members generally. Such mandates as student testing, curricular provisions, instructional methods, and reporting requirements have tended to influence and control the governance of school boards and professional school personnel.

School rating systems in many states have resulted in major pressures on local school principals in the area of student achievement. The pushes on such concepts as performance evaluation, career ladders, high-performance schools, no child left behind, innovative schools, and others have permeated school operations. Such program provisions are some group's idea of something that is preferred, more effective, more humane, less costly, or more just in the matters of school policy; each program reflects a voice that bears upon political action. The political party of such events tends to come and go with new elections and new persons in political offices causing educational leaders to undue and re-due their program provisions.

Many factors have forceful effects and new demands on school governance and policy focus on new issues and new needs. Drug issues, bullying, student dropouts, and teenage promiscuity are examples of such new or ongoing social issues. This combination of concept and event creates a powerful stimulus for the behavior of authority and adds to the turbulence and complexity of school politics in the United States. Such issues as student locker searchers, student dress, student speech, and "loyalty" issues (i.e., flag salute, standing for the national anthem) have had direct effects on school procedural regulations. Student diversity has come more into play. Student discipline procedures, without question, are based on political rights of individuals as well.

Herrity (2010) stated that "the era of change in our communities is accelerating due to the dramatic increase in power groups opening inside local communities. . . . Future gains or rewards are determined by the nature of your interaction with the power network. As a community member and advocate who supports improved lifestyles, it is highly desirable to possess the skills necessary to be successful with community power actors. Such skills are needed in order to minimize potential conflicts and maximize access to valuable resources" (p. 2). Thus, it is of great importance that educators ask the questions, "Are we talking only to ourselves?," "What actual channels do I have for feed-in to assess community signals?," "With whom do I really need to communicate?," and of considerable importance is the question "What do I know about the school community that really counts?"

So, where do we stand? It is clear that education in America is subject to the same realities of political conflict that shape every other aspect of our national life. In the past, school leaders had a more limited constituency consisting primarily of the school board and the local PTA. Today, they are responsible to a much larger electorate; power blocs, each with their separate interests, are often in conflict. The political scene in education is always evolving.

Those who have the major influence on educational matters are reluctant to give it up. As stated by Herrity (2010), "The most successful strategy for a community leader is to recognize who are the power actors in their community and identify the source of their power base" (p. 1). Local school control today requires that school board members and school administrative leaders have the political know-how of being able to identify the internal and external politics that assuredly have an impact on the work of the school system. This means that school leaders must be able to perceive the school system's organizational and political reality and then be competent in dealing with it effectively.

The implications of the foregoing statement focus on the importance of understanding community power dynamics that influence forces of change, policy controls/influences, patterns of decision-making, and the allocation of resources within the community. It is clear that school administrators must develop appropriate political skills in order to survive. School leaders need to ask themselves: (1) Who are the prominent leaders in the community whose "feed in" I need? How can they be identified? (2) How do these leaders go about exercising their power? (3) What are the latent power sources that influence the decision-making process in the school community? and (4) What is the power structure model in this community? Is this the one reflected in the current school board?

It is not that education does not give appropriate consideration to giving its publics a voice in the process of developing effective polices that focus on viable goals and objectives, but education must not abandon its professional prerogatives by regarding educational decision-making as a free-for-all in which education is turned over to others. Although a physician's patient may complain about symptoms and may even aid in the doctor's diagnosis, the patient cannot prescribe the cure or complete the surgery.

In the same sense, the citizenry is entirely within its rights in complaining about school deficiencies and insisting on having an input as to what it visualizes as an end product. The publics can help make a diagnosis by specifying the symptoms and suggesting possible areas of vulnerability. But it is the professional educators' role to translate demands and establish goals for educational improvements that can be programmed with the necessary support required to achieve them.

The new politics of education in America require a willingness to enter into the public arena to promote educational programs required for educational improvements. It means additional participation in decisions by those who are paying the bill as well as other publics that believe that have been outside a "closed system." It underscores the vital importance of participating in the activities known as the politics of education: knowing and understanding how important decisions are made in the school community, including who makes them. This condition means that educators must assert their claims of professionalism by demonstrating knowledge and skill relative to the ongoing political activities that are ongoing in the school community and blending these professional practices in a sincere response to the public with an assertion of the proof of expertise.

One major inhibitor of fostering an open climate in public schools is the limits placed on administrative and teacher personnel for speaking publicly on educational issues and problems facing them. That is, communication on school matters all too often is left mostly in the hands of a single public relations spokesperson or the school superintendent when members of the school community want to hear from the school principal and classroom teachers. As one principal stated, it seems that we are to be held totally responsible for the education of many students but are not seen as being capable of speaking publicly on school matters, including problems that need to be resolved. "Come in, my door is always open" is seldom seen on the door of school superintendents today.

STAFF TRAINING FOR SCHOOL PRINCIPALS, TEACHERS, AND OTHER STAFF PERSONNEL

School leaders must ask themselves if the various staff members are alert to the signals that indicate a need for attention. The local school might not be receiving the immediate feedback from persons who operate at the cutting edge of policy decision-making. In many cases, communication with all voters is overlooked. Parent association members are not the only voters on educational matters. Local school staff personnel are in constant touch with students, parents, and members of the communities in which they live. Keeping the staff fully informed of the issue(s) at hand is of paramount importance.

What about the district's school board members? Is the school board in tune with the realities of the political world of which they are a part? Reality tells us that it is impossible to be thoroughly rational and effective on all issues. Yet, the leadership of the school superintendent and school board members necessitates: (1) an assignment of priorities—we submit that the most important responsibility of the school board is to develop and implement effective school policies for which effective administrative regulations can be developed; (2) attention given to an analysis of relevant variables— such factors must be considered in the decision-making process; (3) a meaningful consideration of the various forces that would be affected by each option in mind; and (4) an assessment and evaluation of the potential consequences of the selected decision. How does the chosen option affect school and community members?

PERSPECTIVES OF POWER

The persons in the power structure need not be office holders, but commonly include individuals who wield power behind the scenes. In many cases, school leaders are communicating with the "lieutenants" and not the "generals" within the community power structure. Although execution of policy takes place within an official group, the formation of the decision might be taking place outside the local board itself.

Growth and mobility have had their impact on community consensus building. The impact of our great mobility has reduced the importance of the neighborhood for over the fence communication and consensus. Fewer local home-owned businesses and corporations are found in our communities as well. Absentee ownership has grown over the years. Top management carries prestige power, but many business managers live outside the immediate school district. For example, these influentials often have a business in a city but live in another city away from the local scene. The children of these business leaders commonly attend schools outside the area of their parents' businesses.

Local school problems are compounded further by the fact that many persons are convinced that the problems of society cannot be resolved by educators. Whenever educational agencies are unable to solve problems through their delegated powers, authority is channeled to higher levels of government or to ad-hoc groups such as business councils, state committees, study groups, and other agencies; thus, local school governance control is further eroded.

We noted previously the views of school practices as being basically unstable: one that drifts unmindful of the environment in which they operate. Some persons contend that educators spend too much time talking to themselves and that the closed system has resulted in an isolation from real issues facing the school community. As a result, the calls for "choice" in the selection of educational options have developed nationally in the force of charter schools, home schooling, online education, and other options now common in our nation.

Even the presence of local school boards has been challenged. Some authorities have noted that the nation is on the verge of what may be considered a constitutional change in the governance of education in America. Education's isolation has resulted in an aloofness to the realities of education's political environment. One authority pointed out that educators are among the poorest judges of the power structure in school-communities.

International competition in space exploration and technology developments over time has radically altered occupational status rankings and priority among competencies needed to implement public policy. Such essentially political forces at the national government level have demanded appropriate responses from schools, regardless of any previous patterns that exist between the schools and the federal government. In turn, the federal government presses hard upon the schools to attend to the various social and academic problems facing the nation including poverty, racial equality, immigration, student achievement, special needs students, and other areas of national concern.

Political forces have called upon the schools with the expectations that education will serve as a change agent for national policy. For example, such programs as those provided for the disadvantaged students were pressed upon the local schools at a time that education was not geared to this phase of need. In the early 1960s, for example, very few schools were prepared to offer programs in special education. Teacher preparation for such programs was limited at best. In spite of the fact that we are able to point to many improvements in educating special needs students and improved academic programs in many schools, the fact is that many social problems such as student dropout rates, racial unrest, academic scholarship, student citizenship, and others remain unresolved.

The word has spread that education in America, although it has improved, has resulted in providing solutions too little too late. Programs such as Common Core came into practice during the Obama administration. Education was told that, although our education was better in the second decade of the year 2000, that it had failed to meet the challenges of the day and so it was out of phase with reality. Although opposing forces of Common Core were strong, it took a complete change in the nation's leadership governance to quiet federal voices for a national curriculum.

In an era of constant change, school leaders benefit if they possess the skills necessary to be successful with community power influentials. Power and influence must be understood by school leaders if they are to understand and manage diverse pressures and demands. By doing so, not only can school leaders gain support for needed projects and programs, but such skills also serve to avoid possible conflicts that might otherwise occur. In addition, the access to valuable resources is a common outcome of power structure analysis. *Power structure analysis* is concerned in general with the distribution of social power among groups in a community that influences decisions and decision-making and how these groups and individuals work together to get things done. The concept of power analysis is discussed further in chapter 2.

The concept of power is viewed from many perspectives. One view focuses on how individuals and groups use their influence to establish guiding policies and regulations and to determine how the resources of the community are to be allocated. Such influence is commonly referred to as *political power*. A related concept centers on organizations and the forces that bring continuity throughout the system to meet desired ends. The term *micropolitics* is viewed as the ways in which power is implemented by individuals and groups to influence the organization's decision-making process in order to achieve the desired goals. *Macropolitics,* on the other hand, refers to how power is used at the various levels of governance, local, state, and federal, to influence decision-making results.

Nearly four decades ago, Thornell (1981) concluded that school superintendents need to know their community power structure's type and areas of influence, and also need to develop better communication techniques with their local power structure. In his study, school superintendents were found to believe that their personal power structure techniques were inadequate. It was found that superintendents preferred to communicate with community power through school-connected channels rather than third parties. We conclude that this feeling remains constant with school leaders today. We found little or no attempts on the part of school superintendents to identify the power structures in their local school community; the most influential member(s) of the school board tended to dominate the attention of these school leaders.

In a number of cases, school superintendents stated that they join local civic clubs under the impression that community influentials are members of such clubs. In other cases, superintendents made efforts to get to know a local banker, director of the chamber of commerce, or business leader in the community not really being sure that these persons were the "generals" in the community power structure.

How Do School District's Policy Manuals Reveal Decision-Making Authority?

What about school district policy development? Most commonly, school policy manuals contain the work of the state's school boards association. As a result, most every school district in the state has the same school policies and administrative regulations. It is not that such policies are not well written or even applicable to the school district's purposes; rather they do not evolve directly from the specific culture of the school community, or they do contain the involvement of the school district's personnel and the input of the school district's citizenry. As a result, the policies remain stagnant in a manual that gathers dust on the shelves of the school's staff or unread on the web established by the school district.

The terms *collaboration, team building, communication, involvement,* and *participation* are used commonly to describe the needs for building effective organizational development in an organization. Purchasing school policies from external agencies inhibits the attainment of these necessary functions. We contacted several school administrators, mainly school principals, relative to their involvement in the policy and administrative regulation development of their school district's policy development and implementation processes. None of these school personnel indicated that they were ever directly involved in the policy and administrative regulation processes of their school districts.

Norton (2017) recommends specific ways in which the foregoing procedures can be improved. The recommendations of the school superintendent are important. Minutes of the past school board meetings can reveal potential policy needs. Suggestions and problems of various school and citizen committees might prompt policy needs. Results of work on the school district's mission and vision statements most likely suggest policy provisions. Employee grievance reports and negotiations that commonly uncover problem areas needed policy clarification. Oft-occurring issues and problems by the school board lend evidence that directive policies are in order, and evaluation and assessment results commonly hold implications for purpose and procedural direction.

Norton recommends ten steps for accomplishing the task at hand:

Step 1. Examine various school and community documents and resources for information relative to what policy decisions already have been determined. Include such sources as school board minutes and correspondence, board and staff committee reports, newspaper files, state statutes and federal mandates, and legal documents related to school district activities.

Step 2. Check on established practices in educational administration and operations of former school boards and often reflect embedded practices that imply policy need areas. Unwritten policies are often the basis for newly written policies for current goals and objectives.

Step 3. Investigate what other school boards have done in the development of school policy. Such information can serve as a guide to possible policy development rather than being directly applicable to the local school district in question.

Step 4. Examine the minutes of the past school board meetings to determine what intended policies might already have been determined. The school policy manuals, handbooks, and policy writings will give clues to important policy topics that have implications for the school district.

Step 5. Enlist the aid of all concerned including citizen groups and education personnel from other school districts. Such involvement is conducive to quality results.

Step 6. Organize study groups to examine policy needs and to participate in helping people perform the related tasks recommended in steps 1 through 5. Establish a steering committee consisting of the most knowledgeable persons to serve as a liaison with study groups in checking for consistency in the policies suggested.

Step 7. Have the school superintendent and administrative cabinet review the policy work completed.

Step 8. Have the school board review the "completed" policy work. The board as a whole should review the semifinal policy drafts and make recommendations for revision.

Step 9. Having the policies examined for compliance with the legal statutes helps to build school board and district confidence and lends support to the final policy package.

Step 10. Use first and second readings of the school board policy statements prior to official adoption. School board policy is legally binding for all school personnel and thus is a contract between the school board and its personnel. Keep clearly in mind that the adoption of school policy is strictly the responsibility of the school board as a whole. Thus, steps 8 and 9 of the recommendations will require ample time for the school board to examine the proposed policies and revise and add policies that the school board finds necessary. As inferred in step 9, having the school board attorney or other qualified legal office examine the policies prior to any adoption actions is of primary importance.

IDENTIFYING LEADERSHIP STRUCTURE

An analysis of the characteristics, status, and relationships related to influential groups and associations commonly results in revealing the following data. Note the low-level rating of education in steps 3, 4, and 5.

Identifying Leadership Structure

1. Characteristics of influential community leaders

    (a) Persons with college training
    (b) Persons in the higher-income brackets
    (c) Behind-the-scene owners of several enterprises

2. Areas of activity

    (a) Local government
    (b) Business enterprise(s)
    (c) Civic affairs

3. Levels of influence   (Scale: 10 high to 1 low)

    (a) Elected/appointed persons in politics. 7.20
    (b) Labor leaders. 6.20
    (c) Civic leaders. 6.16
    (d) Recreation/sports owners. 5.64
    (e) Local government positions. 5.55
    (f) Business enterprise(s). 5.41
    (g) Religious groups/activities. 5.33
    (h) Educators. 5.00

4. Level of status of community leaders (1.0 scale)

    (a) Politics. 50
    (b) Civic. 32
    (c) Labor. 26
    (d) Local government. 18
    (e) Business. 15
    (f) Religion. 06
    (g) Education. 01

5. Frequency of contact with the community leaders (number of contacts per day)

    (a) Politics. 10.1
    (b) Civic leaders. 9.2

(c) Local government. 8.0
(d) Business. 7.8
(e) Labor. 6.9
(f) Recreation. 6.9
(g) Education. 5.2
(h) Religion. 4.7

NEW DIRECTIONS FOR EDUCATIONAL PRACTICES FOR DEVELOPING AND IMPLEMENTING SCHOOL POLICIES

The work on the restructuring of mechanisms for educational decision-making must change. School districts must be able to attack problems of national scope and importance. The new structure must be such that it shares policy making with other agencies involved and effected educational program practices. This need means that school leaders must accommodate other interests in their work. The present decision base of the superintendent and school board, parent groups, teachers' associations, and state school board associations will not suffice. Wide participation is the name of the communication process today.

In an open school climate, the following essentials are present: (1) the school superintendent is knowledgeable of the various school-community services and is involved in the various aspects of community life, (2) the quality of openness is demonstrated by the school's sincere interests in gaining the participation of community members in the work of the school, and (3) the school board focuses on the development of school policy and leaves the discretion of school superintendent and professional staff to develop appropriate administrative regulation for implementing school board policies.

A BRIEF LOOK AT JUDGES OF POWER STRUCTURE

A report completed several years ago by Kimbrough (1964) pointed out that, next to certain minority citizens, educators are the poorest judges of power structures. So, who were the best judges of influential in the school community 50+ years ago? Kimbrough's findings of the most accurate judges were as follows:

1. News media (most accurate)
2. Bankers
3. Physicians
4. Business owners

5. Lawyers
6. Women leaders
7. Laborers
8. Clergymen
9. Farmers
10. Educators
11. Certain minority personnel

Little evidence is presently available that would greatly change the foregoing findings of 1964. The results suggest several appropriate steps at this point and time. Although major changes have taken place in such occupations as farming and medicine, the literature gives little support to educators as astute politicians. First, educators need to be far more realistic and open about the closed-door positions that exist in all too many school districts today. Second, both more effort and money, not just lip service, is needed regarding meeting the needs of our changing world mobility, expansion of knowledge, and individual differences. More emphasis on what we are doing about these realities looms important. Third, educators must begin to communicate in the best sense with our clientele, including those persons who have been identified as most knowledgeable of community influentials.

Several key questions serve to focus on the forces that shape education policy. How is policy developed and implemented in education? Who is commonly influential in deciding education policy? What venues are used commonly by individuals and groups to influence policy adoption? What gives these individuals and groups the power to influence policy matters? What forces within and outside the school district are commonly involved in the decisions concerning what policies will be adopted and those that will not be considered?

It is clear that the days are gone when the local school board and school administrators make the decisions about education alone. Many more agencies, groups, and individuals have demanded a significant role in decisions about education policy and ways in which policy is to be carried out in organizations, and public schools are no exception. In addition, past efforts to isolate social issues such as desegregation, poverty, drug abuse, health issues, rights, and privileges have not succeeded. Matters relating to economics and related national issues have permeated education directly and have challenged the control of educational program provisions as well.

Part of the strategy is gaining the support needed for the plan itself that the school leaders have in mind or gaining the resources needed to implement the plan is the fact that the solution to the plan is the one being discussed and sold to the voters. One wise man said, "If you know the solution, then sell the problem!" All too often, there is a tendency to sell the solution and fail to be sure that the voters understand the problem. When the constituencies understand the problems being faced, then many different solutions are likely to look good to them.

ENHANCING COMMUNICATION
WITHIN THE COMMUNITY

All too often, educators use a commonsense approach and wonder why others cannot see their viewpoint. It must be kept in mind that educators' common sense does not necessarily make sense to one not trained in the education field. The utilization of such approaches as a citizens' seminar can be an effective way to enhance understanding. Study guides and films that point out existing problems can result in gaining citizen suggestions. For example, if the citizens were shown the school districts building status and asked their ideas as to the solutions to and assessment of them, understanding and engagement could be enhanced. One could move from the seminar stage to larger assemblies where citizen reports are given and opinionnaires are administered.

One school district used selected community persons from various groups and businesses to serve as the school district's bond issue committee. Although the school superintendent served as an advisory member of the committee, a local business executive served as the chair of the group. Each member of the committee learned the problems related to school facility needs and, in turn, became a reference person for explaining the importance of the bond issue for retaining the quality of the school programs to members of their own businesses and organizations.

In the foregoing example, one member of the bond issue committee was a reporter of the local newspaper. Another was manager of the local radio station. Helping all members of the committee and the problems being faced by the school district enabled each person the opportunity to receive the data and gain the facts relative to the school needs at hand. Being in the know is a key strategy approach. A person's vanity wants to know before being approached for support. No administrator today should be surprised as to the defeat of a bond issue or school budget override. If such is so, he or she has not done his or her homework.

Developing an effective set of conflict management skills is always important for dealing with critical issues. Being sensitive to the needs and tolerances of the school community serves the purpose of channeling one's energy into the areas which count. The question what does the community want looms important. Getting to know the community means knowing something of the community power structure, getting to know community leaders, visiting and observing them, and visiting them on issues. Reportedly, many leaders say that school people do not see them. Much of the reason for this criticism lies in the fact that most school leaders, including teachers and school principals, are restricted from meeting with individuals and speaking with groups on school matters. As previously mentioned, training is important.

LEARNING TO KNOW THE COMMUNITY

Interestingly enough, school leaders tend not to know a great deal about their community. It might be expected that a school superintendent or school principal new to the school district would not be highly knowledgeable of his or her school committee. However, experienced administrators have been known to possess limited information about their community as well. Empirical evidence suggests that chief school administrators lose their jobs most often because of their inability to deal effectively with the community rather than a lack of academic competence.

KEY CHAPTER IDEAS AND RECOMMENDATIONS

- Current and ongoing issues facing public education, previously assessed and resolved at the local school level, have become state, federal, and special interest group matters as well. The greater the diversity of political action surrounding any issue or problem, the less probable will be the continuation of low-pressure politics for the implementation of educational policy.
- As long as public education is supported by public funds, politics will affect school policies and practices.
- The public has taken seriously the plea of educators to get involved in education. The results are reflected in increasing the desires of the citizenry to focus on education policy matters and demand participation in the decision-making process.
- New issues confronting the nation and local communities have increased calls for the improvement of teacher efficiency and better preparation programs for aspiring school administrators. The importance of knowing the school community and how decisions are reached necessitates new attention to knowing the community in which a school resides.
- Various types of power structure exist in every school community. It looms important for school leaders to know the influential persons who constitute the power structure and determine the policies that will or will not be considered. Empirical evidence and basic research have revealed that educators

are not well informed about the power structure or the persons who are most active in determining policies that determine educational practices.

- Power structure analysis is a skill that must be acquired by school leaders in order to identify the community power structure and establish a communication strategy that ultimately enforces the ability to gain public support for receiving the resources needed for an effective educational program. Educational decisions are greatly influenced by external groups and influentials in the power structure.
- Students, teachers, and staff personnel rights have been upheld by federal laws and court rulings. These rights have strong implications for the decision-making process in the local school system.
- State and federal interventions have led to a reduction of local school control. In addition, power groups have brought about a specific need for school leaders to be knowledgeable and skilled in the identification of community influentials. School leaders must understand community dynamics that influence community change. Decision-making cannot be turned over to other parties, and so they must be able to use strategies that serve to identify and utilize the power influentials for educational purposes. In reality, educators are reluctant to get involved in political matters; it can become "rough territory."
- Governance of education is ever changing, and this makes the application of power structure analysis an ongoing responsibility. Knowing the community is the basis for gaining a knowledge of the community and its present issues and needs.
- Communication has always been viewed as the sine qua non of best practice. However, new strategies must be implemented that serve to keep school leaders abreast of an ever-changing community.
- It is recommended that specific requirements on the topics of the politics of education and power structure be required in each administrative preparation program offered in higher education.

DISCUSSION QUESTIONS

1. Research results have reported that educators are low on the list of persons who are knowledgeable of the power structure in the school community. Set forth several reasons why you believe this finding is true.
2. An individual asks you about the process of power structure analysis and what the process entails. Briefly write out your response.
3. To what extent have the topics of education politics or community power structure been discussed in your school or in other educational settings?

To what extent do you believe you and/or your administrative supervisors are knowledgeable about the topics of educational politics and community power structure?

4. In your school system or in a school system for which you are most familiar, how would you label the kind of power structure revealed by the local school board? What evidence can you provide that would tend to reveal that the power structure is elite, factional, pluralistic, or inert?

5. As a hands-on experience, arrange a meeting with a local official, business leader, office holder, or other community leader. Develop four or five questions that you will ask the person about the community power structure or related matter that centers on a political decision made or is being voted upon. Write a paragraph or two about what you found most interesting and informative.

Case Study 1.1   The Behind-the-Scenes Campaign

The Silver Springs Institute was a nonprofit organization that operated on the motto of "Educational Opportunities for All Children and Youth." It was administered by non-educators and owned by three of the wealthiest persons in the Epmet City School District. The Silver Springs Institute had lobbied effectively for state financial support on the bases that it was serving special needs children and youth in its charter schools that were not under the supervision of the state department of education. The institute argued that the public schools were not doing justice to students with disabilities and that the institute, with state financial support, could enroll and meet the needs of kids with disabilities.

Effective lobbying, along with providing campaign financial support for state legislative candidates, overtime, had resulted in the election of several Silver Spring Institute supporters to the state legislature. Silver Spring Institute officials, along with the wealthy owners of the institute, were able to gain the support of the state legislature in the passing of a bill that gave $10,000 support funds for each student who entered the educational program of the institute. Over time, institute monies resulted in the passing of a bill that included state financial support for all students who enrolled in the institute's program.

Although charter schools, under the state's educational supervision, had to report on budget matters, including the use of state funds, other educational schools, such as the Silver Springs Institute, were not required to do so. Nevertheless, a close investigation by news reporters and other officials of the state revealed that the state monies given to the institute for special needs students were being mixed with general fund

monies obtained by the Silver Springs Institute from tuition fees, contributions, and other funds that were viewed as dark money provided by
supporters of school choice and other individuals who were owners of
the institute.

Protests of the state financial support given to the institute were vocally
contested by public school supporters. No accounting of income and/or
expenditures of the institute were ever mandated by the state government.
In fact, the governor of the state argued that the institute's program was
meeting the state laws relative to school choice. The governor indicated
that he would be in favor of financial support for all schools of choice,
including private and parochial schools. The state governor had been supported financially during his candidacy for office.

Although the institute voiced its high student achievement record,
objective evidence of student testing was not made available for public
scrutiny. Inquiries by outside sources for information regarding student
achievement, enrollment requirements, educational expenditures, or
acceptance of minority or low-achieving students were ignored. Calls to
the institute for information related to enrollment requirements, numbers
of special needs students, salaries for institute personnel, including the
executive leaders of the institute, went unanswered.

Case Discussion

Although the name of the institute and the city in which it existed in the
case study are fictitious, the basic politics of the case are based on an
actual situation. Consider each of the following questions in a group setting or give individual thought to each of them.

1. As a teacher, administrator, or citizen in your community, what is your
   definition of school choice? To what extent, for example, should a public, private, charter, or parochial school be operated outside the juris-
   diction of the state in our opinion?
2. To what extent should any K–12 school program be under the supervision
   of the state? That is, what should be the parameters under which a school
   of choice be operated in a democratic society?
3. Why, in your opinion, should public school programs be "controlled"
   by the state? Or, in a democratic society, should school attendance
   and operation be left strictly to the decision of parents and/or state
   governments?
4. What factors, in your opinion/experience, have led to the growing
   voice of school choice and private ownership?
5. Which statement seems to define the status of public education today?
   "The Politics of Education," or "Educational Politics"? Or, are these two
   statements synonymous?

REFERENCES

Dahl, R. A. (1958). A critique of the ruling elite model. *American Political Science Review*. New Haven, CT: Yale University Press.

Domhoff, G. William. (2005). Basics of studying power. (webpage). *Who Rules America?* University of California Santa Cruz. On the web: https://whorules america.ucsc.edu/methods/studying_power.html.

Herrity, J. P. (2010). *Understanding community power structures*. Consulting Solutions for Organizations. West Des Moines, IA: Preferred Visions.

Hobbes, T. (1651). *Leviathan*. Later published as *Leviathan* by Thomas Hobbes, C. B. Macpherson (Editor, Introduction), Penguin Classics on November 19, 1981.

Hunter, L. (1953). *Company power structure*. Chapel Hill: University of North Carolina Press.

Kimbrough, R. B. (1964). *Political power and educational decision-making*. Chicago, IL: Rand McNally & Company.

McCarty, D. J., & Ramsey, C. E. (1968). Community power, school board structure, and the role of the chief school administrator. *Education Administration Journal Quarterly, 4*, 2, 19–33.

Norton, M. S. (2017). *A guide for educational policy governance: Effective leadership for policy development*. Lanham, MD: Rowman & Littlefield.

Richmond, E. (2017, August 7). The trump effect on Canada's classrooms. Boston, MA: *The Atlantic Magazine*.

Petress, K. (2015, December 18). *Power: definition, typology, description, examples, and implications*. From the web: http://utshcsaedu/ . . . /PowerDefinitionsTypolo gyAExamples.pdf

Root, E. (1998, May 1). Lincoln as a leader of men. *Social Media Monitor*. Ashland, OH: Ashland Center, Ashland University.

Thornell, A. L. (1981). *The influence of the community power structure on school board decision-making*. ERIC, Eric Number: ED202163. East Texas School Study Council, Commerce.

Wirt, F., & Kirst, M. (1982). *Schools in conflict: The politics of education*. Berkeley, CA: McCutchan Publication Corporation.

Xavier University (2016, July 29). *Student lobbying, political and campaign activities policy*. Cincinnati, OH: Office of Student Involvement.

Chapter 2

Boards, Governments, Organizations, Associations, and Other Groups: Politics of Education and Policy Development

Primary Chapter Goal: To explain the complexity of politics and its influences on public school programs and operations.

THE POLITICS OF LOCAL CONTROL

Chapter 1 centered on the fact that education is involved in the politics of decision-making and the influences that various power structures play on educational programs and practices. In this chapter, the political impacts on education by internal and external forces, such as local, state, federal governments and other political operatives, are detailed.

The fact that the power structure of the local school board commonly reflects that of the local school community was noted in chapter 1. In summary, empirical and basic research have shown that an elite or dominate community power structure is represented in a local school board when one member of the board tends to dominate the decision-making process. In addition, school board members are re-elected time after time. In the decision-making process, voting is always decided on a unanimous basis. Most commonly, school board members look to one of its members for final decisions on important policies.

The factional type of power structure at the local school level is more political. It is more divided and the leadership authority of the board depends on the issue at hand. Thus, the school superintendent is more of a political strategist and is using his or her best diplomacy to keep positive relations with members who are divided on issues themselves. It is common for voting to be divided as well; 5 to 4, 3 to 2, voting is the common practice. We note

here, however, that the school superintendent of this and other power structure boards feels comfortable and satisfied in the specific administrative role.

The pluralistic power structure, as noted in chapter 1, is more open. Democratic principles are evident on the part of the school board and school superintendent. The school superintendent serves as an advisor to the board. For
example, the superintendent commonly gives his or her advice on issues that
the school board considers and often recommends needs and actions for the
board to consider. Lengthy discussion generally precedes voting on an issue,
but unanimous voting generally takes place.

Inert school board power places the board in a "rubber stamp" position.
That is, the school superintendent commonly drafts a policy, he or she
presents the policy to the school board, and the board sanctions the policy
unanimously. Thus, the school superintendent is the decision-maker in this
situation. Nevertheless, in cases of issues for which the board members are
vitally concerned, the board has been shown to demonstrate their authority
for or against the proposition at hand.

We review the local school power structures here since control of school
decision-making within each of the four power structure types has been
altered by the interventions of state and federal authorities. That is, school
boards in the United States have had to assume the role of compliance bodies. School boards are directed to carry out the mandates of state and federal
governments and also the rulings of the federal courts.

The role of the chief state school officer is becoming increasingly political,
with the rise of tough accountability standards and mounting tension over
the funding of charter schools (DeNisco, 2013, p. 1). Reform does not come
easily. In order to realize needed educational changes, state education leaders
must activate political actions that gain the cooperation of unions, national
and state school boards, state legislators, wealthy influentials, and other foundations and groups that have interests in education.

POLITICAL TUG-OF-WAR AND EDUCATIONAL
PROVISIONS: A CASE IN POINT

A recent case in one state serves to underscore the political forces that operate
in most every educational decision of paramount importance. "Actors" in the
educational decision process included the voters, the courts, the state governor, parents, lawmakers, public education advocates, special interest groups,
attorneys at law, teachers, and public school retirees. The political matter
centered on the question of expanding the state's voucher-style program.
In an article by Sanchez (2018, March 22), it was reported that the state's
Supreme Court had ruled that voters would get to have a vote on whether or

not the state's current school voucher program should be done away with or be expanded.

Sanchez noted that mostly a group of grassroots parents and public education advocates called for and won a decision to place the matter on the ballot. This decision by the state's Supreme Court upheld an earlier ruling by a lower court and served as a major setback for supporters of the voucher system. It is beyond the scope of this chapter to discuss the complete details of this political "battle" in education, but it serves to underscore the total involvement of various parties in educational matters. What is not known at this time is the unknown power influentials that won or lost in the Supreme Court's decision. What "generals" above the actors in this case were active and influential in the final decision is a question of interest and importance.

STATE POLITICS AND THEIR INFLUENCE ON LOCAL SCHOOLS: THE POLITICS OF WHO SHOULD CONTROL EDUCATION

At the state level, decision-making does differ among the 50 states. However, figure 1.1, set forth in chapter 1, demonstrated a common arrangement for the various forces acting upon the educational policy-making process in education. The figure does represent the general power structure of public education in most states. What figure 1.1 does not show is the behind-the-scenes power groups and individuals that also are engaged in educational policy-making. The figure illustrates the common flow of decision-making in the state and local school districts. State responsibilities, "inferred" by the U.S. Tenth Amendment, have changed over the years from service to oversight, and today have centered on regulatory and compliance measures.

The controls placed on local education by the state legislature, the state governor's office, and state board of education have increased via state mandates and federal legislation that changes to a great extent with each new presidential administration in office. For example, the argumentative Common Core mandates, that intervened during the Obama administration, declined as the Trump administration moved into office. The implementation of many federal mandates is optional in some instances. However, if a school district needs federal monetary support, compliance predicts additional local controls.

Researchers, such as Kirst (1988), attribute the reduction of local control of education to such factors as the loss of confidence in the public schools to provide quality education. Issues related to civil rights, student rights, closed school climates, teacher rights, and multicultural issues were viewed as being overlooked in local school politics. As these issues became more important

Table 2.1   Judgment on the Quality of America's Public Schools: Your Grade

GRADE	5/91 %	6/06 %	4/18 %
A	8	13	____
B	22	36	____
C	30	32	____
D	12	9	____
F	8	5	____
Don't Know	20	5	____

in state and federal programs, local school teachers' associations and parent groups tended to lose influence. Other social and economic factors, such as declining student enrollment, the student dropout problem, local taxation issues, increasing property taxes, and related court issues regarding student rights, were causes of the reduction of local initiative and power influence.

Jacobsen and Saultz (2011) reported on a Gallup poll that revealed the grading of America's public schools by Americans in 2006. Table 2.1 reveals the grades given according to percentages for 1991 and 2006. Now, we ask *you* to take a minute and record your personal opinion of the quality of public schools in 2018, 12 years later.

How does your grading compare to the grading of Americans 12 years ago? Do you believe that the grades given by Americans in 2006 would be higher if another 2018 poll were administered? Why or why not? We do note that 81 percent of the American participants in the poll gave public schools grades of A, B, or C in 2006. The A to C grading percentage of 81 percent in 2006 was 21 percent higher than in 1991, a significant improvement. For purposes of comparison, two polls, 2007 and 2016, were examined in an article by Peterson and others (2017). In brief, the poll results for the grading of public education by the general public in 2007 and 2016 gave 22 percent grades of A or B in 2007 and 24 percent in 2016.

POLITICS AND SCHOOL BOARDS

Norton (2017a) points out several conditions surrounding the work of local school boards that inhibit their ability to maintain a leadership position for the local control of education. For example, the majority of school boards in America continue to purchase their school board policies from their state's school board association. These boilerplate procedures not only supplant the board's decision-making authority, but they also inhibit the ability of staff personnel to become committed to the desired school aims and objectives. In addition, empirical evidence underscores the fact that many school boards and professional personnel lack the required knowledge for distinguishing between policies and administrative regulations. The difference between these two terms serves to distinguish the division of labor between the elected or appointed school board and the hired professional staff personnel of the school district.

Few educators are aware that there exists a Politics of Education Association that has been in operation for fifty years. Its mission strives to foster research and support the conduct, dissemination, discussion, and application of research on the political functions of education at all levels, with the final view of contributing to the betterment of society. In any case, local school districts have tended to surrender policy development to state legislatures and others such as the state association of school boards. Local school policy manuals in most states today are products of the state's school board association. Thus, local control is unavoidably reduced for establishing the purposes of education in the local community.

Titles of the Politics of Education Association's yearbooks reveal its political research interests. Among its many yearbooks are *The Politics of Curriculum and Testing, The Politics of Teacher Education Reform, Curriculum Politics in Multicultural America, The Politics of Teacher and Administrator Preparation and Professional Development, and The New Politics of Education.* We note this information for the purpose of underscoring the ongoing influences of politics on educational matters. For example, the association's yearbook on accountability (Jacobsen & Young, 2017) reveals these phenomena:

(a) accountability policy has expanded the number and diversity of political actors; (b) accountability policy has contributed to shifts in traditional alliances; (c) political actors are using traditional and new strategies to influence and respond to accountability policy; (d) accountability policy has altered institutional structures and norms, shifting distribution of power and resources; (e) accountability policy creates more accountability policy; and (f) the focus on performance-or test-based accountability has contributed to a decline in democratic accountability. (p. 155)

Norton (2017a) recommends that school boards work to become power leaders as opposed to power followers. One way to accomplish this need is for school boards to take control of the policy development in their school districts. In fact, this is a school board's primary responsibility. Bell (1988) suggests that this can be accomplished by boards if they become assertive policy-makers who direct administrative and management functions by setting forth the broad purposes and ends that the school district is to achieve. In turn, the school board gives needed discretion to the professional staff for administering the regulations for accomplishing the desired ends.

Political power does not take place only because of the authority assumed by the position held. In the case of school boards and local control, serious attention must be devoted to becoming effective policy decision-makers which, in most cases, will require effective training in policy development. In addition, school board members must become knowledgeable and skilled in the area of politics and power structure. Cooperative efforts between and among teachers' and administrators' organizations, parental groups, local government officials, and other groups and individuals must prevail. Otherwise, local school boards will continue to be acting as compliance boards for implementing mandates set forth by external agencies.

Ideally, there would be a mutual agreement between the state and local school districts for establishing the broad purposes of education, refining the broad purposes of education to meet the special needs and interests of the state's school districts, and then leaving the refining of the broad purposes of education to local school districts for defining the aims and the means for accomplishing them.

POLITICAL ADVANTAGES AND DISADVANTAGES
OF STATE CONTROLS OF EDUCATION

Killian (1984) and others have identified various advantages for increased state control of education. For example, authorities have pointed to the interventions of state and federal government educational support for students with special needs. Both social equity and needed financial support have been credited to state and federal sources for such purposes.

State legislatures have been especially supportive of establishing equitable tax programs for educational purposes. Financial ability to pay for effective education programs has been found to differ in a ratio of 6 to 1. That is, the richest states in the union are six times more able to pay for the education of a child than the poorest states nationally. Equalizing a student's access to education regardless of his or her geographical location is not only fair but also necessary.

A strong argument for state control centers on the quality differences that have been found in educational programs throughout the states. Education reforms in Texas and other states have legislated major reforms for the improvement of educational programs. Such mandates have been among the most argued measures that states and federal requirements have projected; standardized testing and Common Core provisions are primary examples. Yet, failing schools have been eliminated and ineffective school administrators have been dismissed in some cases.

On what bases do state legislative personnel decide on important legislative matters?

Empirical evidence suggests that legislators give thought to the bill sponsors, the status of thinking of party leadership, input from lobbyists, communication with fellow legislators, and the thinking of constituents. An article by Canfield-Davis et al. (2009, August) studied this question and found that legislature representatives' decision-making on bills depended on personal feeling, constituent desires, recommendations of colleagues, staff recommendations, input from interest group views, and recommendations from friends when asked about school issues.

THE FAR-REACHING ARM OF COMMON CORE

Without question, the most controversial state intervention into local school educational programs sponsored by the National Governors Association (NGA) and the Council of Chief State School Officers (CCSSO) centered on establishing educational achievement standards for students in all states. For example, the standards for mathematics laid out the domains for teaching mathematics in each grade from K through 8. Measurements and data were required for grades K–9 and geometry for grades K–8. The mathematical content to be taught in grades 9–12 was not specified; however, conceptual categories of content to be covered at the high school level were defined (e.g., number, quantity, algebra, functions, modeling, geometry, statistics, and probability). Standards for English language arts included reading, speaking, and listening; language; and media and technology

Of the 50 states, 42 became members of the Common Core State Standards (CCSS) initiative, but not without both support and criticism from politicians, analysts, commentators (Wikipedia, 2017, December 22) and school administrators, teachers, and parents. It has been noted by Wikipedia that, as of May 12, 2015, three states had reported the repeal of Common Core. Nine additional member states had legislation in some stage of the process that would repeal Common Core participation. Like many enforced mandates, their positive features leave some positive benefits to the operations of school programing. Much of its other chaff falls through the cracks of ever-moving educational change.

Tighter state controls of education are viewed as being disadvantageous for a variety of reasons. The most frequent argument for reversing state control is the contention that educational needs and interests are best determined by persons closer to the home of the student. A solution for gaining more local control has been the trend toward educational choice by way of voucher systems that support charter schools, home schooling, and financial support for private schools.

Other arguments for and against local control of education often are cited. Each argument carries with it historical, cultural, legal, and political implications. Nevertheless, some forces argue that local control can: (1) improve

efficiency and in turn reduce educational expenditures by effectively organizing the inefficient district operations exemplified by consolidating school
districts and eliminating inefficient and unneeded offices, improving costly
purchasing practices, and centralizing ineffective operational functions related
to maintenance and other district operations; (2) reorganize and consolidate
rural school operations and the small neighborhood schools that are operating
inefficiently in many school-communities; (3) eliminate the many bureaucracy barriers that exist in many city school districts that inhibit efficiency
in the decision-making process; (4) implement effective policy development
processes within the school district that focus on important educational goals
and require higher academic standards for student learning; and (5) open the
concept of state, national, and global education that extends opportunities for
learners to be able to participate intelligently in other multicultural communities encountered in today's mobile population.

Arguments for retaining and increasing local control include: (1) keeping
the education of children and youth close to home is important since parents,
teachers, administrators, and school board members are the persons closest
to and most interested in the students' welfare and (2) participating in the
improvement and support of the educational program is facilitated in schools
that are controlled primarily by citizens of the local school community. Our
children, our schools, our goals, and our values are protected when local
control is in place.

So, even at this point and time in history, it is difficult to determine who
is actually the primary decision-maker for public schools. The politics and
debates as to how the resources (funding) are to be paid and distributed continue. If charter schools are to continue to grow, who is to pay for them and
who is in charge? Smarick (2016) gives a simple (if messy) answer to the
question by saying, "No one and everyone" (p. 2). Nevertheless, he raises a
major question that definitely needs a better answer than we are witnessing
in practice today, "What is the best way to arrange a city's system of schools
given our tradition of local control and the state's ultimate obligation of
responsibility?"

It seems that a working arrangement between the local school districts
and state offices is a reasonable answer to the question, "Who is in charge of
education?" Uerling and O'Reilly (1989) targeted one absolute reality to the
question of control. As these authors point out:

> Local control of education is a concept that has become embedded in American
> culture. It is generally accepted that decisions about the education of children
> in a public school district should be made by those who are closest to the site.
> However, major policy decisions about education are not made at the local
> school level; they are made by legislative bodies, both at the state and national,
> and in some instances by state courts.

Local boards of education have long had the responsibility for assignment of students, by grade and location. Still, that authority has been conditional and stipulated by the judiciary as well as federal and state statutes. Boards commonly have control over admission, of students to their local schools, but they may not deny admission to handicapped children or assign students by race. Boards have control over hiring and assignment of staff but cannot be prejudiced or biased in any of the eight categories of protected citizenship in such board actions. Boards are responsible for fixing the compensation for teachers, but in most every state, statutes demand that boards engage in collective bargaining with faculty. These fluctuations are in authority over public education and demonstrate how closely state and local authority interrelated. . . . Public education is not a condition of state government vs. local government, although some board members and some legislators may sometimes see it as so. (pp. 1–2)

FEDERAL POLITICS AND EDUCATION ARE INEXTRICABLY LINKED

The federal government has a lengthy history of involvement and concern for public education. "Such influences were embedded in the actions of the First Continental Congress 233 years ago in the passage of the Land Ordinance of 1785" (Norton, 2018, p. 1). Two years later, Thomas Jefferson drafted the Land Ordinance of 1787 that declared that the No. 16 lot of every township be reserved for the maintenance of public schools. History shows that the federal government was mainly responsible for creating a public school, and this action opened the path for public education that spread toward the West. From that time on, national legislation during the administration of the nation's 44 presidents, public education was a national concern.

PUBLIC SCHOOL LEGISLATION OVER THE YEARS AT THE NATIONAL LEVEL

From the earliest history of the seventeenth century, schools were being opened and education was indeed on the minds of the colonist leaders. As a member of the Continental Congress, George Washington was instrumental in passing legislation that established the Land Ordinance of 1785. This legislation took place two years before the United States Constitution was signed on September 17, 1787, and ratified approximately nine months later on June 21, 1787. This date was approximately six months before the very first state, Delaware, was ratified for joining the Union. From that time on, our nation's presidents, some far more than others, have set forth their views and contributed positively to public education. Selected contributions will be presented in a later section. Political implications surround each entry.

AN OVERVIEW OF THE FEDERAL
GOVERNMENT'S EDUCATION LEGISLATION

We note the article on the federal role in education to set forth a brief history of federal involvement in education (ED.gov, 2017). The original U.S. Department of Education was created in 1867 to collect information on schools and teaching that was intended to help states establish school systems. The department has changed its name and mission several times over the years. Besides focusing on effective teaching, vocational education, education for students with disabilities, math and science programs, physical health and welfare also have been among the many concerns of the federal government.

The early passage of the Morrill Act and the Second Morrill Act in 1890 gave major impetus for establishing land-grant colleges and universities nationally. As previously noted, vocational education has been a primary federal concern as demonstrated by the 1917 Smith-Hughes Act and the following 1946 George-Barden Act that centered on agriculture, industrial arts, home economics at the local school level.

Many school districts benefited by the Lanham Act of 1941 and other impact laws of the 1950s that supported the burden placed on them by the military presence in their school districts. Support payments for military-dependent students residing in the school district and monies for the construction of school buildings and facilities were made available by the federal government. The positive educational contributions of the 1944 "GI Bill" cannot be overly praised for its approximate $8 million support for veterans' college education.

The Soviet *Sputnik* launched the federal government's educational involvement in the later years of the 1950s. The "fear" that the United States had fallen behind the Soviet Union educationally led to National Defense Education Act that pushed the schools to step up elementary and secondary school programs in the areas of mathematics, science, foreign language along with addition financial support for vocational/technical education.

Civil rights issues and related concerns during the years of the 1960s through the 1970s saw the passage of the historical Title VI of the Civil Rights Act. Later amendments and legislative acts centered on political issues related to discrimination due to race, sex, disability, and religion. One of the most far-reaching federal acts of 1965, the Elementary and Secondary Education Act, prohibited discrimination of any kind to be unconstitutional. Civil rights enforcement was placed directly on the operation of public schools. The Department of Education by 1980, once again, changed considerably to become present in most every curricular program and practice of state and local school educational governance. Reportedly, the Department of Education increased its presence in most every phase of approximately 18,200 local school districts with 98,000 public schools and 32,000 private schools (ED. gov, 2017).

There is no question regarding the growth of the federal government's involvement in public school education. Despite the criticism of its increase in intervention in public school programs and governance, federal agencies contend that it has not waved from its historical mission of promoting student achievement and preparation of assuring educational excellence and equal opportunity for an access to education. In view of the federal government's Common Core mandates, many states and local school district personnel have strongly objected to the program's mandated requirements for curricular offerings and teaching methodology.

MORE FEDERAL MONEY:
PART OF THE PROBLEM OR PART OF THE SOLUTION?

In an article that appeared in *USA Today* (Danilova, 2018, January 1), the U.S. Commission on Civil Rights reported that too often, black and Latino students end up in schools with crumbling walls, old textbooks, and unqualified teachers. The commission said that inequities are caused by the fact that schools are mostly funded with state and local tax dollars. That is, 92 percent of public school financial support comes from state and local funds leaving only 8 percent to be paid by the federal sources. Nevertheless, the question as to whether federal intervention has had a considerable influence on education policy is an unquestionable answer of "yes." As stated by Jack Jennings, founder and retired director of the Center of Education Policy, "Policy should be integrated into politics . . . decisions will be left to those who are not equipped to make them—or worse, who are simply uninterested in fairness and equity in education" (Limiell, 2012, February 10, p. 3).

The foregoing information by all other reports is substantially true. Assume that 100 percent of the school financial support was equally divided among the local, state, and federal taxes. That is, each of the three government agencies paid one-third of the public school educational budget. What control factors would, without question, result in additional controversy? Federal control historically has been a major problem even though it is financing a low 8–10 percent of the total education budget. Might we conclude that additional federal funding would lead to additional federal control of education?

A SUMMARY OF SIGNIFICANT LAWS,
REGULATIONS, AND POLICIES

The United Federation of Teachers (1999–2017) published a listing of federal laws, regulations, and policies set forth by the federal government. The listing provides a perspective of the federal government's major concerns regarding student disabilities, student civil rights, family education rights, privacy protection, and teacher qualifications. These acts are summarized in order to illustrate the federal government's political interventions into educational programs at the elementary and secondary school levels. Each entry carries with it political implications and the question as to which level of government holds the responsibility for deciding such educational issues.

In regard to student disabilities, both the local education and state programs receive federal funding. However, federal agencies set forth the program aims and procedures that must be followed if such financial support is to be received. To what extent should the federal government be deciding the qualifications for local school teaching personnel, teacher evaluations, student discipline procedures, student achievement objectives, student bullying, and student transportation requirements? If the answer is that these provisions should be within the authority of the states and the local school community, then the question of supporting them financially through tax assessments is proper.

The federal government's hand is once again revealed in the matters of family education rights and student privacy. What local school can do regarding these issues is mandated in the federal government's Family Education Rights and Privacy Act (FERPA) of 1974. The question is not if the provisions set forth in FERPA are in the best interests of students and students' families, rather the question centers on who should be the decision-maker regarding student/family education rights and privacy matters. Who is deciding these matters at the present time is clear; it's the politics of the federal government and its agencies. Thus, federal government is the decision-maker, and the local school board serves in compliance.

WHO FAVORS WHAT IN REGARD TO
WHO SHOULD CONTROL EDUCATION?

It seems clear that the control of public education has shifted from local control to state and federal control over the past five decades. Yet, Jacobsen and Saultz (2011, August 29) point out that the public is less ready to join the shift away from local control. These researchers have found that, while there is some favorable opinion for state involvement in education. a growth in the reservation of state and federal control has become more evident. That is, the majorities of the public tend to favor local control over state and/or federal participation. Jacobsen and Saultz found an increase in the levels of satisfaction with local schools and a slight decline in dissatisfaction.

When asked about their satisfaction with public schools, the majority of the public reported that it wanted to see more influence by the local school districts. Early studies revealed the fact that the citizenry favored state government's "say" about local education; nearly 50 percent indicated that the state had "too much influence." It appears that the favorableness component for state and federal involvement in education relates closely to the extent that such involvement is favored when matters of equity and welfare are apparent in the issue. In any case, although local control of education has been invaded by state and federal legislation and related mandates, public opinion sends a message of strong support for local control.

THE POLITICAL LIFE
OF NATIONAL EDUCATION ASSOCIATIONS

One reference listed 37 professional organizations for K–12 educational leaders (Dyrli, 2017). The listing included the well-known associations of the American Federation of Teachers, National School Boards Association, National Education Association, American Association of School Administrators, National Association of School Principals, Association of Business Officials, and the National Parent Teacher Association. Yet, besides the 37 education associations listed by Dyrli, there must be at least another 37 major educational associations and councils not in the listing such as the American Supervision and Curriculum Department, University Council for Educational Administration, American School Personnel Administrators Association, the Chief State School Officers Association, and the American Educational Research Association along with the several hundred education associations active at the state and local levels.

We note the number of existing educational associations and councils since each one represents a political force in education decision-making even though their primary purposes center on educational development and improvement. As an example of the involvement in educational politics, we discuss the activities of three of these national organizations, the American Federation of Teachers (AFT), the National Education Association (NEA), and the Council of Chief State School Officers (CCSSO). The American Federation of Teachers, located in Washington, D.C., approximates a membership of 1,600,000, assets of $106,404,940, and employees numbering 460. The Federation was founded in Chicago approximately 100 years ago.

Wikipedia (2017) reported that in 1998 the membership of the larger National Education Association rejected a proposed merger with the AFT. The history of the AFT is marked with the series of teacher strikes during the early to late 1940s and later in the 1960s and 1970s. Each such occurrence resulted in an increase in the Federation's membership and political involvements. Albert Shanker served as the president of AFT for a twenty-three year period of time that began in 1974 and ended in 1997.

During his tenure as president, Shanker was an advocate of charter schools, called for competency testing of teaching personnel, advocated merit pay for teachers, and supported high-level requirements for high school graduation. He was especially active in promoting teacher empowerment through the collective bargaining process. Shanker was twice jailed for his political involvement in illegal teacher strikes (Wikipedia, 2017). His problematic political controversies with the National Education Association were ongoing.

THE RECORD OF POLITICAL
EXPENDITURES OF THE AFT

Reports indicate that the AFT provided campaign contributions of $1,784,808.59 to the 2016 Hilary Clinton campaign. Since 1980, the AFT and NEA have contributed nearly $57.4 million to federal campaigns that has been reported as being approximately 30 percent higher than any other single corporation or union. Of special note is the fact that political donations from teachers' unions have gone to Democrats (Wikipedia, 2017). Overall, although exact figures for political campaign spending are not available, such spending has reached into figures of several billions of dollars. Such spending, more than most anything else, reveals the importance of gaining political power by having your man or woman in strategical government offices and positions.

THE NATIONAL TEACHERS ASSOCIATION
AND ITS POLITICAL PROWESS

A recent article (Wikipedia, 2017a, October 31) identified thirty three specific issues of the National Education Association (NEA), which encouraged members to get involved in political activities. At present, the NEA has approximately 3 million members and a budget of approximately $345 million.

NEA's stated mission does not mention its involvement in the nation's politics but specifies the association's interest in advocating for educational professionals and the uniting of members to fulfill its promise of preparing students to succeed in a diverse and interdependent world.

Selected NEA political activities from its inception in 1857 include its early endorsement of women's suffrage, its plea for improving illiteracy nationally, promotion of state retirement plans for teachers, the raising of teachers' salaries, additional federal and state support for education, and other related political activities. From the early 1940s to the 1980s, the NEA supported such programs as the G.I. Bill, the National Defense Education Act, the Civil Rights Act, and the endorsement of Democratic politicians such as Jimmy Carter, who helped to secure the U.S. Department of Education. In later years, the NEA lobbied for such issues as the federal retirement equity law, changes in the No Child Left Behind Act, and expressed opposition on such laws as discriminatory treatment of same-sex couples.

Historically, and in the more recent years, political activities and funding have been focused on assistance of political campaigns almost exclusively for the Democratic Party. In 2015 for example, the NEA endorsed Hillary Clinton for the nation's highest office. Moe (2001) and others have criticized the NEA for what they believe has been NEA's support of teachers rather than students. Other criticisms center around the association's views and/or failure to be more concerned about abusive teachers, sexual abuse, homosexuality, and NEA dues payments whereby teachers have to pay dues even though they do not wish to be members of NEA. The rationale for this provision is that even a nonmember teacher receives the benefits of all teachers when a positive legislative state or federal action is passed with NEA support.

As noted by Birch (2011, December 8), the NEA spends millions of dollars on political lobbyists. For example, state affiliates of the NEA regularly lobby state legislators for funding, seek to influence educational policy, and file legal actions. The NEA's political activities increased significantly since its creation of the NEA Political Action Committee in the 1970s for the primary purpose of getting more directly involved in local election campaigns and endorsing political candidates who actively supported the association's policy goals.

Without question, the NEA's mission, related to several selected purposes, is founded by one primary activity—POLITICS:

Professional educational organization
Opposing financial cuts to education
Lobbying for education
Increasing educational funding

Teachers' rights protected
Influencing state and federal education laws
Collective bargaining rights
Salary equities for teachers

THE COUNCIL OF CHIEF STATE SCHOOL OFFICERS AND ITS COMMON CORE FOOTBALL

If one educational program were to be selected as most controversial, most likely the initial laws regarding taxation for public schools, the racial integration of public schools, the new mathematics of the 1960s, state funding of private schools, collective teacher negotiations, reading instruction methodology, and mandated student testing would be among the top entries. In contemporary times, the Common Core program, led by the Council of Chief School Officers (CCSSO) and the National Governors' Association (NGA), might well be near the top of the most controversial listing. Although most every state in the nation signed up for the implementation of the Common Core Standards for implementation in public schools, at the time of this writing, the status of Common Core was not at all clear.

Not only has Donald Trump campaigned against Common Core but has continued to question the program's contributions to education. The general contention appears to be that Common Core requirements are fading away in school programs nationally. Like most of all such innovations, some of the Common Core's positive characteristics (e.g., improvement standards, focus on effective methodology) are retained in ongoing programs, and other less-accepted requirements tend to fall through the cracks of ever-changing educational program practices.

THE CENTRAL FOCUS AND POLITICAL PURPOSES OF THE CCSSO

The Council of Chief State School Officers (CCSSO) describes its mission as providing leadership, advocacy, and technical assistance on major educational issues. It seeks member consensus on major educational issues and expresses these views to civic and professional organizations, federal agencies, and the public. A primary project of CCSSO has been the implementation of a system for determining content alignment across grade lines and with alternate standards and assessments. Such alignment focuses on the development and implementation of comprehensive standard-based education systems that link content standards, curriculum, instruction, assessment, and professional development to guide student learning in achieving educational goals.

Once again, the primary focus of the CCSSO efforts has been to gain alignments with the curricular program standards and the testing instruments used to assess that goal. The dollars, research, and efforts devoted to this project have been significant. One reference listed twenty-three reports that the Webb Alignment Tool (WAT) produced. Many states had used the WAT by the year 2005. The primary purpose of detailing the CCSSO efforts here centers on its goal of controlling the curricular standards for public school programs and student learning. It is difficult to determine the impact of CCSSO's efforts today; changes in the political goals of the new Trump presidential administration and the U.S. Department of Education most certainly will determine its ultimate fate.

THE NATIONAL PTA POSITION STATEMENTS

The political influence of the local, state, and national parent-teacher associations is reflected in its impressive membership numbers. Their voting numbers, coupled with the voting numbers of teachers, give these associations a high level of political power. Historically, local school district PTAs have changed from social groups that have moved from donating funds for purchasing school stage curtains to involvement in the decision-making policies and procedures for public schools nationally. The involvement of parental groups in matters of education is being revealed in their ongoing communication with legislative representatives, their school boards, and their constant presence at sessions where important educational matters are being discussed.

The political power influence of the PTA is not merely an outward force focusing on state and national legislation, but it has been highly concerned about the quality of local school education programs and the low level of student academic achievement. We keep in mind that the PTA, like all other associations and organizations, has its detractors as well as its supporters. For example, the PTA has been criticized, on one hand, for interfering into school matters that are best left to the professional education personnel. On the other hand, criticism has been directed toward the PTA for being no more than a "pawn" for the teachers' association.

Some criticism has been directed toward the PTA for its lack of political clout. It is unable to support publicly "education" candidates for office positions due to its tax-exempt status. To do so would jeopardize this status. Perhaps the PTA's political focus can best be explained by examining its list of national position statements on educational student and program matters.

Seven specific position statements have been set by the National PTA (PTA, n.d.) as follows:

Each major PTA position statement includes *selected topics* of concern:

1. *Child Health*

   Early identification and intervention for children with mental health needs
   Nutrition for children and families
   Recommendations regarding prescription opiate abuse awareness and prevention

2. *Child Safety and Protection*

   Positive student discipline
   Recommendations on corporal punishment
   Trauma-informed care

3. *Educational Technology and Student Data Privacy*

   Mass media
   Student data privacy and security
   Gun safety and violence safety

4. *Elementary and Secondary Education*

   Arts in education
   Assessment
   Teacher preparation and staff development
   The principal as the school educational leader
   Prayer in schools
   School choice

5. *Gun Safety and Violence Prevention*

   Firearms
   Gun safety and violence safety

6. *Opportunity and Equality*

   Citizenship and equality
   Rights and services for undocumented children
   Shared responsibility in decision-making
   U.S. Supreme Court decisions regarding segregation

7. *Special Education*

   Education of students with special needs

Each of the foregoing entries is "defined" and/or explained additionally in the book's glossary. For example, the entry of educational choice is explained as follows: The National PTA supports public school choice and acknowledges *educational choice* for public charter schools as one of the many avenues for improving student achievement. However, the charter school's program must reflect the positions and principles of the National PTA. One criticism of the PTA has been its tendency to hang on the coattail of the teachers' associations. As one critic stated, "As goes the teachers' union, so goes the PTA."

TAXPAYERS AND FINANCIAL REFORM

The calls for more involvement in and control of schools have not been restricted to parents. The taxpayers have placed political pressures in a variety of forms: (1) the pressure being placed on states to assume more responsibility for financing education; (2) the ways in which school funds are distributed for financing education; (3) the setting of tax ceilings for funding school costs; and (4) the financial state support given to private schools and some programs in parochial schools. The politics of determining "who pays" is problematic at best. The "formula" is quite clear: ISF + ILF = IUT: Increased State Funding plus Increased Local Funding equals Increased Unwanted Taxes.

DESEGREGATION, IMMIGRATION, INTEGRATION

Desegregation has been evident in the political scene effecting educational policy of the United States historically. Every area of the country has been influenced by various coalitions of interest groups, legal rulings, and the media. The matter of the educational services being provided to minorities and enhancing their life opportunities has been an ongoing political issue.

The involvement of all of the various publics in desegregation and its related issues brought several truths to the forefront. The greater the diversity of public involvement in the politics of any social/governmental area, the less likely will be the continuation of low-level politics. And the greater the stress such participation of diverse publics places upon various issues and groups, the less likely is it that consensus will be realized.

Whereby, in the past, political consensus was more easily reached and conflicts resolved through extralegal networks, these informal means have long ago disappeared and more formal bodies such as legislatures and courts have risen to determine just what matters were to be decided about what was to be done about them. In addition, influential corporate executives, in the past, were most commonly also members of their child's school community. Their interest in the local issues of education in the community was far more personal. Today, the determination of corporate policy is decided from a long-distance basis, and the corporate leader's interest in the education of the school district has become far-distanced and passive.

The point is, of course, that education has been forcibly moved farther from local policy decisions and more to the political arena with other agencies that vie for the same public dollar. Historically, members of the school board have been "well-known" business men and women. This fact is no longer the case. A community parent, former school teacher, or individual who was working in a small business in the community are quite likely to be a candidate for the local school board. It is not that such persons are not capable individuals, but most likely they are not among or well acquainted with the influential members of the local power structure.

Previously, we discussed the matter of students and their rights. Unilateral administrative handling of student matters is no longer tolerated and certainly not politically astute. Student rights developments have added new dimensions to the once-unchallenged policy authority of school personnel. There are many other major factors directly affecting school governance. These forces are less discrete than those previously discussed, but nevertheless these factors have had direct and far-reaching effects on what schools do and how its professionals must act.

The economy, for example, weighs heavily upon resources available and decisions as to how these resources are to be distributed becomes a political matter that extends from the federal government to state and local school policy affairs. The availability of jobs, the contemporary illegal immigrant problems, and economic competition internationally have become major political concerns. Various governmental agencies have generated many new demands on education. These demands are mandated in a variety of forms, including mandates, rulings, laws, and court rulings.

Many of these demands have become part of the ongoing procedures of school districts nationally. Such demands constitute a new force from a variety of new constituencies placing some restraints on the former professional dominance of local school programs. A lessened local control of education has been the result. Another political influence is that of the invasion of new concepts that center on social change. For example, such concepts as career ladders, increased teacher performance evaluation, language-learner programs, and mandated instructional approaches have penetrated school classrooms when incentive funds are made available by federal and state agencies. The point is that the large majority of such interventions are brought about by external political forces, not singularly by the local school board.

Every such program, action, or activity is someone's idea of something that is viewed as being more humane, less costly, more just, of more quality or more effective by some party. Each view reflects a biased voice that bears upon political action. Various issues and events are among the many factors that have a forceful effect on the demands of school governance and policy. Those who have the power are reluctant to give it up; those who seek it often overestimate their knowledge and/or skill to do so.

The use of illegal drugs by young persons, teenage promiscuity, AIDS, bullying, saluting the flag, and other such issues are examples of events and concerns that gain much attention and result in extended conceptions as to how the educational values are to be attended. This combination of concepts and events creates a powerful stimulus for the behavior of authority and adds to the turbulence and complexity of school politics in the nation today. As one principal commented, one problem for him is that many of the mandates that come to his desk tend to change from month to month or year to year.

INFLUENCES ON EDUCATION OF SPECIFIC MOVEMENTS IN AMERICA'S HISTORY

It is beyond the scope of this chapter to discuss all of the various eras that have had direct influence on educational program practices. Nevertheless, the era of progressivism serves to demonstrate the impact of such movements on the political, social, economic influences of educational reforms. The era of progressivism has been identified in some references as prevalent during the years of 1880 to 1920; other references give the era a much earlier time and other a much later time in history. Still others indicate that the features of progressivism are still operational in America's educational philosophy. Our focus will center on the definition of progressivism and its political influence on education.

The term *progressive* was engaged to distinguish this education from traditional Euro-American curricula of the nineteenth century, which was rooted in classical preparation for the university and strongly differentiated by social class. By contrast, progressive education finds its roots in present experiences (Wikipedia, 2017b). Selected qualities for most progressive programs include emphasis on learning by doing, strong emphasis on problem solving, group work and social skills, understanding as opposed to rote learning, collaborative and cooperative learning projects, education for social responsibility and democracy, personalized student goals, community service and a look to skills needed for the future, emphasis on lifelong learning, and assessment by evaluation of learner's projects and productions.

Progressive education can be traced back to such world leaders as Johann Hebart, John Dewey, Maria Montessori, and Friedrich Frobel who created the concept of kindergarten. John Dewey, a United States leader of progressive education, set forth his concepts of progressive education in his answers to what education is and to what the school is, the subject matter of education, the nature of method, and the school and social progress. For example, in answering the questions of what education is and what the school is, Dewey stated that education should take into account that the student is a social being and that the school should be a form of community life; the school is part of society and should reflect community life.

Gutek (1986) notes that the basic themes of progressivism were addressed in the following six frames: (1) Government should regulate economic power in the public interest; (2) Expert knowledge and the scientific method should be applied to solving social, political, economic, and educational problems; (3) The national environment should be conserved and its quality enhance; (4) Political institutions and processes should be reformed to make government more efficient; (5) The spirit of community should be revitalized in the burgeoning urban areas; and (6) Educational institutions and processes should facilitate democratic participation and scientific efficiency (p. 200).

PROGRESSIVE POLITICS THAT
HAVE INFLUENCED EDUCATION

Progressivism was revealed and practiced in many different ways in education. Laws concerning child labor, restrictions in child labor, poverty, social justice, business-like efficiency in school matters, the application of scientific principles, and the rise of criticism that education was being dominated by politics were among the characteristics of progressive concerns. Educational reform was foremost in the progressive movement during the early 1920s.

Of course, the focus on efficiency was prominent throughout the scientific management era and education was not an exception. Frederick Taylor's concepts of scientific management entered all fields of educational practices (Taylor, 1915). There was no greater criticism for a school or school leader than being inefficient. Being efficient meant applying the scientific managing principles set forth by Taylor: (1) a structured management process was required whereby the supervisor was responsible for planning and supervising the work, and the worker was to carry out the plan under controlled procedures, (2) the plan set forth the distributing of minute, specialized tasks that, when taken together, would get the job done more efficiently, and (3) relating the small tasks to such practices as time and motion studies that would serve to increase production when put into practice by the workers. Control was the name of the game.

The influence of the scientific management practices became widely accepted by school leaders nationally. School leaders, for example, were to be viewed as chief executive officer (CEO) of the school system, a title that was welcomed by administrative personnel. Administrator conferences soon adopted the concept as was illustrated by the session topics presented in such professional meetings. Such topics as "The Principles of Scientific Management Applied to the Teaching of Music," "Setting and Maintaining Efficiency in the Teaching Force of Normal Schools," and "A Study of Adolescent Efficiency" were among the various conference topics (Callahan, 1962).

The political impact of scientific management's control concepts during 1900–1920 could be compared to that of the more contemporary impacts on schools as the pressures for mandated curricular standards and achievement testing. Both movements waned after a period of time but left their mark on educational program practices. For example, in the case of scientific management, the terms *job descriptions, division of labor, span of control, incentive pay, bureaucracy, accountability* and many others are present today in education practices. We contend that the terms *learning standards, achievement testing, effective schools, school mission and vision, special needs, collaboration* and others will continue to find their way in education programs in the years ahead.

Today's politics of education require a willingness to gain the knowledge and skills required to compete in a world of competitiveness relative to the resources needed to meet the ever-changing requirements facing education. The accomplishment of this goal depends in large part on the ability of educators to assert their just claims of professionalism and upon their skill in blending a sincere responsiveness to the public revealed in the proof of expertise and competitiveness in the ongoing politics of decision-making. Chapters 3 and 4 focus more directly on developing such required skills.

CHAPTER POST-TEST

Directions: Circle your answer for each of the following first ten multiple-choice questions and then answer true or false for questions 11 through 15. Check your answers with the correct answers set forth at the end of the post-quiz.

1. The power structure of the local school board has been found to

    a. be a pluralistic or a democratic type of power structure.
    b. be impossible to determine since some board members change most every year.

c. reflect the same power structure of the local school community.

d. be missing approximately 85 percent of the time.

e. be none of the above.

2. The school board with a factional school structure commonly would be

    a. more democratic.

    b. more political.

    c. more effective.

    d. more efficient.

3. Authorities have placed the ongoing loss of local control of education on

    a. a loss of confidence on the part of the citizenry.

    b. the failure of the school in providing quality education.

    c. issues surrounding civil rights differences.

    d. the closed system of public schools; lack of openness.

    e. multicultural issues.

    f. none of the above.

    g. all the above.

4. School policies and school administrative regulations are

    a. synonymous.

    b. different.

    c. interchangeable.

    d. under the jurisdiction of the local school principals.

    e. most effective if developed by agencies outside the school district (to avoid bias).

5. Overall, it is a best practice to

    a. keep education out of politics.

    b. keep politics out of education.

    c. become knowledgeable and skilled in the area of politics.

    d. leave the matter of politics to the state legislature.

    e. hire an expert in the area of politics to handle all political matters.

6. One strategy for gaining more control of school policy matters is

    a. increasing the trend toward school choice.

    b. reducing the federal government's 69 percent of public school support.

    c. eliminating the federal department of education.

    d. appointing rather than electing school board members.

    e. requiring college degrees and professional business experience for serving on the local school board.

7. The early first and second Morrill Acts focused on

    a. establishing private and religious schools in the several territories.
    b. requiring all parents to pay school tuition for K–8 school instruction.
    c. mandating that each territory reserve lot 16 for the establishment of a public school.
    d. establishing a kindergarten program in each elementary school established in the territory.
    e. none of the above.

8. Which entry below has not had political influences on matters of public education?

    a. PTA
    b. NEA
    c. CCSSO
    d. FTA
    e. scientific management
    f. Progressive Era
    g. all entries have had political influences on matters of public education
    h. none of the entries have had political influences on matters of public education

9. The CCSSO had a major part of promoting which of the entries below:

    a. The Morrill Act of 1785
    b. Common Core
    c. No Child Left Behind
    d. The U.S. Elementary and Secondary Education Act
    e. Title IX of the Ninth Amendment to the U.S. Constitution

10. _____ has/have been evident in the political scene effecting educational policy of the United States historically.

    a. Desegregation
    b. Research strategies
    c. Citizen apathy
    d. Power structure knowledge and skills
    e. Strong financial support of public education

True or False?

11. A strong argument for state control of education centers on the quality differences that have been found in education programs throughout the states T_____ or F_____?

12. One way for school boards to accomplish the role of power leaders is to take control of policy decisions in their school districts. T____or F____?

13. Although differences between local, state, and federal agencies have occurred on many occasions, all three governments tended to favor the Common Core Standards program of the Council of Chief State School Officers. T____or F____?

14. Even at this point and time, it is difficult to determine who actually is the primary decision-maker for public school policies/programs. T____ or F____?

15. Educational practices today might be far more advanced and effective, but the early colonists gave little concern to the topic of public education in their deliberations. T____ or F____?

ANSWERS TO POST-TEST

Answer to Q-1 is "c," reflect the same power structure as the school community. If the school-community power is inert, research shows that the school board will most likely be the same kind of power structure. The school superintendent is active in recommending policy provisions and the school board acts to approve them.

Answer to Q-2 is "b," more political. A factional school board is more divided on educational issues than other school boards and political strategies are used by the board members who are proposing a new policy for adoption. Voting on an issue most commonly results in a split vote.

Answer to Q-3 is "g," all of the above. Each of the entries has had a strong effect on the loss of control by the local school board. Overall, the public has tended to lose confidence in the public school to do what is needed in the educational program for student learning.

Answer to Q-4 is "b," different. A policy is a general statement that serves to answer the question "what to do." It leaves discretion for determining administrative regulations that answer the question "how to do."

Answer to Q-5 is "c," best to become knowledgeable and skilled in the area of politics. Education's involvement in the matters of local and worldly affairs results in it being directly involved in the political decision-making processes that affect the ways in which the resources and values of society are determined.

Answer to Q-6 is "a," increasing the trend toward school choice. This answer is not to recommend the concept of choice as a best procedure, but rather to underscore the fact that choice tends to provide options for educating students and satisfying the political opponents of public education.

Answer to Q-7 is "c," mandating that each territory reserve lot 16 for the establishment of a public school. This early legislation was of great importance for assuring the continuation of public education in America and also reflected the fact that the early colonist leaders were aware that a democracy could not be retained without an educated citizenry.

Answer to Q-8 is "g," all of the entries have had political influences on matters of public education. This chapter has demonstrated the fact that education, like all other organizations, is directly involved in the competitive world of power and political decision-making.

Answer to Q-9 is "c," the Common Core. The CCSSO was the primary organization that established the concept of Common Core Standards for public school curricular provisions and methodology for their implementation in the classroom.

Answer to Q-10 is "a," desegregation. The matter of equality and access to public education has been on the agenda of American policy historically. Who is to be educated and other matters of student rights have been among the major decisions of the United States Supreme Court.

Answer to Q-11 is "True." Equity in educational opportunities and availability to quality education, historically, has differed greatly from state to state and school district to school district. The ability to pay for quality education differs among the states as well. Thus, the federal government's involvement in public school matters has focused on resolving such inequities and mandating student rights relative to educational opportunities.

Answer to Q-12 is "True." Local control of policy development carries with it a high level of local control of educational programs decision. Thus, having boilerplate policies written by the state school board association delegates authority to that agency. In addition, the purchasing of state board policies overlooks the value of local participation in the decisions that directly influence administrative and classroom practices.

Answer to Q-13 is "False." It must be stated that the majority of states did commit to the use of Common Core programs, but many later withdrew and, at present, the Common Core provisions have been set aside by most school districts.

Answer to Q-14 is "True." The involvements and influences on public school decision-making presently are so divided among the local, state, federal, and other external agencies and forces that "control" are quite difficult to define. Among the "confusion" is the recent governmental changes at the presidential and educational levels. It is not that the local school boards do not continue to operate, rather the present enforcements of program standards remain cloudy.

Answer to Q-15 is "False." In fact, the early colonist leaders gave education considerable attention. George Washington, Thomas Jefferson, and other early governmental leaders were well aware of the fact that a democratic republic could not be sustained without an educated citizenry. The point here is that the colonists and early U.S. presidents did view public education as being of paramount importance and did take steps to establish public schools in the territories.

KEY CHAPTER IDEAS AND RECOMMENDATIONS

- Public school education is involved in the politics of policy decision-making and the influences that various internal and external agencies, groups, and individuals play educational programs and practices.

- The controls placed on education by state legislation, governors' offices, and federal agencies have increased substantially over the years as demonstrated by the most recent Obama administration and actions such as Common Core supported by the Office of Chief State School Officers.
- Loss of confidence in the local schools to meet contemporary education issues and needs has led to a reduction in local control of education programs and practices.
- The contemporary practice of using boilerplate educational policies developed by the state school board association has added to the reduction of policy-decision making at the local school level. School boards must become policy leaders as opposed to policy followers in order to retain some semblance of local control.
- It is recommended that a mutual agreement be established whereby the state legislatures set forth broad guidance purposes for education and then hold the states responsible for defining the procedures and processes for meeting them.
- Common Core is one primary example of external agencies "forcing" local schools to waive their local control of program curriculum and instructional methods. Local school control can be in force only if the local school board does not have the authority to make program.
- Local control does have both benefits and related problems. The best compromise is for the states to set forth the broad aims for public education and allow the local school authorities to tend to the best local applications of these goals and objectives.
- There has never been a time in U.S. history when the federal government has not shown its "concern" for public education. The status of vocational education, support of education for meeting the educational needs of children with special needs, desegregation of schools, and other such interventions have demonstrated federal concerns historically.
- The progressive movement within the United States has had its impact on educational philosophy. Its external influences on education are revealed in many ways in contemporary educational practices today. External forces will continue to influence decision-making at the local school level. Thus, it is of paramount importance for public school leaders to become knowledgeably involved in the ongoing issues facing the world and take the necessary steps to initiate positive program change.

DISCUSSION QUESTIONS

1. Review the chapter section on progressivism and its primary concepts/characteristics. Then, identify those concepts/characteristics that are

apparent in contemporary education. To what extent are any of the Progressive Era concepts apparent in current practices?

2. What events, influences, and issues brought about the Progressive Era? Explain how each of these factors changed or influenced education in America.
3. Select one individual that contributed substantially to the Progressive Era. Identify two or more of his or her concepts that remain in contemporary education.
4. Consider policy development in your school district or one for which you are most familiar. Determine the answer to the question "how are school district policies developed/established." For example, what person(s) or group(s) actually write the policies for the school district?
5. Consider the influence of the PTA, school-based council, or similar group in your school community. How would you judge their effectiveness in the educational decision-making process? Which term best describes the group's political influence on educational program matters: Highly effective? Somewhat effective? or Ineffective?
6. Assume that you have been asked to explain your professional opinion on the federal involvement in education at the local school level. Take a few minutes to think about what your response will be. Then write out the primary points that you will address in your response.
7. If at all possible, list or find out about the last several education policies or major program decisions that were adopted in your school district. In each case, do your best to determine the person(s) or group(s) that were the foremost supporters of each policy. Was the school board the primary decision-maker behind the adopted policy? Were they the same persons or groups for each policy? Factional groups? State legislative mandates? Or other support factions?
8. The primary goal of this chapter was to underscore the complexity of politics on public school programs and operations. To what extent, in your opinion, was this goal realized? What evidence would you submit to support your opinion on this matter?

REFERENCES

Bell, T. H. (1988). Parting of the 13th man. *Phi Delta Kappan, 69,* 400–407.
Birch, B. A. (2011, December). NEA spends $133 million on lobbyists. *Education News*. From the web: www.educationnews.org/category/education-policy-and-politics/
Callahan, R. E. (1962). *Education and the cult of efficiency.* Chicago, IL: University of Chicago Press.
Canfield-Davis, K., Jain, S., Wattam, D., McMurtry, J., & Johnson, M. (2009, August). Factors of influence on legislative decision making: A descriptive study. *Journal of Legal, Ethical & Regulatory Issues,* 13(2), 55–68.

Danilova, M. (2018, January 11). Poverty, segregation persist in US schools, report says. *U.S. News.* From the web: https://www.usnews.com/news/politics/articles/2018-01-11/poverty-segregation-persist-in-us-schools-report-says.

DeNisco, A. (2013, September 15). Politics seeps into school leaders' role: Accounting standards charter school funding sometimes causing controversy. *DA District Administration.* Trumbull, CT: Privacy Policy.

Dyrli, O. E. (2013, August 15). *A list of professional organizations for K-12 leaders.* Organizations provide solutions networking and professional development. Trumbull, CT: Privacy Policy.

ED.gov (2017). *The federal role in education.* /print/about/overview/fed/rol.html

Gutek, G. L. (1986). *Education in the United States: An historical perspective.* Englewood Cliffs, NJ: Prentice-Hall, Inc.

Jacobsen, R., & Saultz, A. (2011, August 29). *Trends—Who should control education?* The Education Policy Center. East Lansing: Michigan State University.

Jacobsen, R., & Young, T. V. (2017). The new politics of accountability: Research in retrospect and prospect. *Education Policy,* 27(2), 155–169.

Killian, M. G. (1984). Local control—The vanishing myth in Texas. *Phi Delta Kappan,* 66, 192–195.

Kirst, M. W. (1988). Who should control our schools? *NEA Today,* 6, 74–79.

Lamiell, P. (2012, February 10). How should politics influence education policy? *Teachers College Newsroom.* New York, NY: Columbia University.

Moe, T. (2001). *Special interests: Teachers unions and America's public schools.* Washington, DC: Brookings Institution Press.

Norton, M. S. (2017a). *A guide for educational governance: Effective leadership for policy development.* Lanham, MD: Rowman & Littlefield Publishers.

Norton, M. S. (2017b). *Dealing with change: The effects of organizational development on contemporary practices.* Lanham, MD: Rowman & Littlefield Publishers.

Peterson, P. E., Henderson, M. B., West, M. R., & Barrows, B. (2017). Ten year trends in public opinion from the *EdNext* poll. *EdNext Journal,* 17 (1), Winter.

PTA (no date). *National PTA position statements.* Lindsay Kubatzky, Governor Affairs Coordinator. From the web: https://www.pta.org/home/advocacy/pta's—positions/Individuals-Positions-Statements

Taylor, F. W. (1915). *The principles of scientific management.* New York, NY: Harper & Row.

Sanchez, Y. V. (2018, March 22). Voters to get say on expanded vouchers. *Arizona Republic,* p. 1A.

Smarick, A. (2016, April 4). *Local control versus state obligation.* Washington, DC: Thomas Fordham Institute.

Uerling, D., & O'Rielly, R. (1989). *Local control of education.* Nebraska Policy Choices. Miles T. Bryant, Patricia O'Connell, and Christine M. Reed (eds.). Omaha, NE: Public Policy Center.

Wikipedia (2017). *Common core implementation by states.* From the web: https://en.wikipedia,org./wiki/common-core-implementation-by-states

Wikipedia (2017a, October 31). *American federation of teachers.* Washington, DC.

Wikipedia (2017b, October 31). *Progressive education.* From the web: en.wikiuniversity.org/wiki/progressive education

Chapter 3

Politics and Power Structure Analysis

Primary chapter goal: To extend the concept of power structure, to establish specific characteristics of school-community power structures, and to present research regarding the identification of power structure and its political implications for application at the local school level.

The nature of power structures existing in school communities was introduced in chapter 1. The identified characteristics of power structures are extended in this chapter, and the research findings of *power structure analysis* are discussed. In chapter 1, the fact was noted that, in many cases, the execution of policy takes place outside a specific group itself. It is common for a small group of the power elite to determine policies that ultimately are adopted by a local group, such as a school board. The operation of power and influence in the school community must be analyzed if the school leaders are to understand and manage diverse political demands and pressures that are bound to occur.

Neighborhood over the fence consensus is no longer a major force in the decision-making process relative to school policy. Political forces are calling upon local school districts to serve as change agents for implementing national mandates. Such forces have brought new pressures upon the role of the school superintendent and school board. New Issues and related problems, facing the nation as a whole, are finding their way to the local school level; the school tends to receive the blame for lack of student achievement and irrelevant curricular offerings. Some persons contend that educators are too busy talking to themselves to be able to be effective in the world of politics.

On his website on power structure research, Domhoff (2005b) lists fifty-five titles in the reference that centers on the topic of power structure. The topic of power structure has been given much attention in the literature; power structure is one of the most controversial topics among theorists and social researchers. Opposing views on the topic of power structure have been set forth by sociologist, political scientists, pluralists, and Marxists. Thus, power structure research results, completed by the reputational theorists, organizational theorists, power structure theorists, and power elitists, have served to keep the topic of power structure controversial and somewhat unclear.

HOW TO RESEARCH THE POWER STRUCTURE OF YOUR SCHOOL COMMUNITY

The goal of power structure analysis is to gain an understanding of how influential individuals go about exercising their power and to find out what issues, problems, and situations are those in which their power is utilized. Perhaps, of most importance is determining how educational leaders can improve their leadership in the area of policy development and program improvement through exercising effective communication with latent power sources as well as being more effective in their own use of power

> Power structure research is a method of analysis based on criticizing unfair systems, structures, and institutions in society. This analytic tool is used by many researchers to study social, political, economic, and cultural practices that create, expand, defend, or restore inequalities of power and privilege based on race, gender, and class. Power structure research unveils the social costs of corporate activities in terms of work, government, policies, quality of life, and the sustainability of a healthy planet. (Berlet, 1968–2014, p. 1)

Power structure analysis all too often is beyond the scope of the school superintendent whose agenda is already overcrowded with administering mandated requirements of the school board, state offices, and federal agencies. Few school districts nationally have effective "scientific" research units in place. Those school districts that do have a research component are not likely to focus on the identification of power structure. Rather, such components commonly are given the tasks of administering the student attendance and retention rates, projecting enrollment statistics, administering quality of service surveys, maintaining current district mapping data to produce accurate boundary maps and, in some cases, actually programming the testing mandates set forth by the school board or the state.

Although such tasks are of importance, they do not contend with matters relating to the politics of education that are foremost in the decision-making processes related to major financial resources distributions that have become locally, statewide, and nationally competitive. Specific strategy activities for determining school-community cultural changes, forecasting forthcoming issues and problems that likely will be faced by the school district, or performing effective power structure analysis that underscores the decision-making processes within the school district are mainly beyond the scope of school leaders' abilities.

Empirical evidence tends to indicate that school boards members are not fully aware of the importance of being knowledgeable and skilled in the political arena. In fact, the actions of many school boards and school leaders reveal the behaviors of power followers rather than power leaders when it comes to policy development; this fact militates against effective decision-making at the local school level. Such evidence is exemplified by the way policy is "developed" in the majority of school districts nationally. Boilerplate policies, developed by external agencies and associations, reveal this fact.

POWER AND POWER STRUCTURE DEFINED

Power and *power structure* have been researched and variably defined in the literature historically. In the following sections of the chapter, selected definitions of power and power structure are discussed relative to the purposes of politics in education. In following up on these definitions, the topics of power and power structure are developed additionally from their introduction in chapters 1 and 2. The focus of this discussion centers on the recommended local school leader's procedures for identifying and communicating with the local influentials in the local school-community power structure.

The importance of such local school communication for school personnel centers on determining the answers to the following questions: (1) Who are the prominent leaders in the school community whose "feed in" I need? (2) How do these leaders go about exercising their power? (3) What channels of communication are most effective for communicating with these influential leaders? (4) What are the latent power sources; the power generals who represent the behind the scenes power sources? (5) What is the power structure (model) of the current school board? Question 5 is important since it is common for the local school board power structure to reflect that of the local community. In an effort to implement the school-community power structure model, in-depth definitions of power and power structure are in order.

The term *power structure* is defined in various ways historically. Several examples of such definitions follow. In each case, give attention to the focus of each definition (e.g., people or groups mentioned, the nature of the structure in which power is based, and the nature of the power itself).

"Power structure" is:

- "the formal and informal social networks by which power is concentrated and institutionalized" (Burris, 2012).

- "the . . . social structure, politics, economic, and cultural practices that create, expand, defend, or restore inequalities of power and privilege based on race, gender, or class" (Berlet, 1968–2014).
- "a group of people who have control of a government, organization, etc., or the way in which those people are organized" (*Merriam-Webster*, 2017).
- "those persons or groups in a nation, city, organization etc. who, through economic, social, and institutional position, constitute the actual ruling power" (*Merriam-Webster*, 2017).
- "a network of organizations and roles within a city or society that is responsible for maintaining the general social structure and shaping new policy initiatives" (Domhoff, 2005b).
- "a way in which power is organized or shared in any organization or society" (*Cambridge Advanced Learner's Dictionary*, 2018).
- "Power is the medium through which conflicts of interest are ultimately resolved. Power influences who gets what, when, and how" (Morgan, 1986).

For each of the foregoing definitions, take note of the factors and characteristics concerning how and where power is concentrated, factors that accompany and/or reveal power, and how the definition focuses on people and groups. When considering the power structure of the local school community, one would logically consider the internal factors of the local school system (e.g., school board, school superintendent, assistant superintendent, department heads, and teachers). The city governance officials such as the mayor and city council would be viewed as external power groups. Other external groups would include the parent-teacher association, chamber of commerce, local media CEOs, and other special clubs and agencies.

However, the latent power structures and power individuals are most likely to be the community generals who have the power resources to control important issues and policies that influence local school operations. *Power structure analysis* is a procedure for attempting to identify these influential groups and individuals.

PERSPECTIVES OF THE TERM *POWER* IN RESPECT TO INFLUENCE AND CONTROL

In the following section, the term *power* is defined additionally as viewed by several references in the field. Bal and others (2008) defined the term *power* simply as "the potential to influence others" (p. 5). The definition underscores the researchers' concept that a person cannot be a leader without having power, but he or she can exert power without being a leader. These researchers go on to describe seven bases of power. We make special note of the fact that position power represents only one of the seven power bases. At the local school level, power usually refers to the ability to establish policies and procedures that serve to fulfill the goals and objectives of a school and/ or school district.

"In social science and politics, *power* is the ability to influence or outright control the behavior of people" (Wikipedia, 2018, January 8). In this sense, power can be perceived as making certain actions possible or it could be to restrain unwanted actions. Other terms associated with power are *upward power* and *downward power*. When the power is vested in the top authorities, it is viewed as downward power. In cases where the power comes from the subordinates of the organization, it becomes upward power. That is, the organization's power comes from the employees; when important policy and/or administrative decision comes from the employees, upward power is in force. Although not used commonly in power discussion, *latent power* might well be termed *quiescent power*. Quiescent power is an influence that is external to the internal organization and not easily identified. It is commonly associated with behind the scenes and enforced by individuals who are often called the power captains.

Several bases of power have been identified. For example, the *power of charisma* is derived from the individual's personal style or personal character traits. It commonly is termed *referent power* and is based on the individual's ability to attract other people and gain their loyalty and respect. *Position power* or *legitimate power* extends from the position in the hierarchy that one holds. For example, the school superintendent asserts more power than the assistant superintendent and other administrators in the school system.

The *power of relationships* is positively gained through the outcomes of positive relationships within a network of friends, colleagues, and acquaintances within or outside the organization. Ongoing and effective communication facilitates the development of trust and openness among the internal and external components of the group and/or organization. *Referent power* is somewhat related to the power of relationships in that it results in influence due to a followers' loyalty, respect, and desire to gain a person's approval. In a somewhat different perspective, power can be increased simply by decreasing one's dependence on other persons.

The *power of information* is that quality possessed by an individual commonly called upon for resolution of a problem or problems facing the organization or group of people. Organizational issues and problems necessitate the knowing of facts that surround a situation. Information relative to such matters is a first step toward problem solution. The person possessing such information is in a position of power.

The *power of knowledge* or *expertise* can serve to influence the decision-making process and provides valid answers for perplexing encounters and organizational issues. The person with this knowledge/expertise possesses the skills needed by the organization. They are able to recommend solutions to problem areas facing the organization. People tend to seek and appreciate this person's knowledge and expertise. When a person "gives" his or her knowledge for ongoing purposes, in one sense he or she lessens his or her power potential. That is, the primary company leader and others in the company begin to know as much the employee who possessed the knowledge originally. Arguably, this result is not a negative factor; the point is, however, that the knowledgeable employee overtime loses the power.

The *power of punishment,* also referred to as coercive power, is vested in the ability to set forth sanctions that negatively impact on the unacceptable performance behavior of other individuals. The ability to withhold rewards or to create a concern that prized rewards will be withdrawn carries an assurance that others will toe the line and/or agree to the wishes of the power holder. The possibility of losing a job or being demoted fosters allegiance on the part of the worker, but resentment and resistance commonly results in practices such as *soldiering* whereby the "victim" goes through the motions of loyalty and high performance but is only marching in place.

Punishment can result in compliance for a short time, but when extended over longer periods of time can result in ineffective behavior. Dysfunctional work behavior and a working atmosphere of dissatisfaction and fear can result which is exemplified in the undermining of production goals and objectives. Soldiering can take place, which presents a false impression of productivity, whereby little real work activity is being accomplished. Threats by management of termination for failure to comply are representative of coercive power. Nevertheless, the worker's complying behavior is underscored by his or her lack of cooperation, creativity, and personal initiative.

Kelman (1958) set forth three basic reactions to coercive power and its influence: *compliance*, *identification*, and *internalization*. In the case of compliance, the workers do comply with the orders set forth by the authority but tend to disagree with them. Unless the actions of the group are not closely observed, the workers most likely will not follow through with the orders. In the case of identification, the worker(s) tends to agree with the authority's orders and carries them out virtually to a degree. If this behavior is continued, internalization results. Internalization takes place on the part of the worker(s) if the given orders are in agreement with their personal beliefs and opinions.

The *power of reward* is found in the ability to reward others for distinguished service and/or meeting high standards in their work activities (Bal and others, 2008). Being in the position of providing a material or verbal satisfaction for "a job well done" adds to the authority of the giver. Financial rewards represent only one dimension of reward power. Many authorities favor such provisions as improved work schedules, promotions, words of praise, time off, and other forms of recognition. Reward systems have been known to lose their motivation incentives when simply given as a certificate to everyone for time in service or being employee of the week.

In the foregoing study, three of the power bases headed the listing; the power of relationships, power of information, and the power of expertise. These three bases each received ratings of 4 on a scale of 0-low to 5-high. The power to reward others and power of charisma each ranked 3.3, while the power to punish others was lowest with a ranking of 2.2. What power sources will be most important in the next few years? The power of relationships was viewed as highest by the participants in the study with the power of information close behind.

One other form of power commonly reported in the literature is *virtual power*. This form of power is developed by cooperative activity within an organization or among organizations to solve a problem through the actions of more than one source. It is evident when two or more sources join together to improve a situation or gain resources that only one source can produce.

Power, as used in this book, is simply being able to develop guiding policies and implement the administrative procedures necessary for carrying out the policies in question at the local school level. This definition makes it necessary for the school leader(s) to be knowledgeable of the school-community power structure.

POWER QUIZ

For each question, select the best or most appropriate answer.

1. Delmar has the ability to give Richard a bonus for work achievements. Elmer has charisma.

   a. True
   b. False

2. Knowledge power tends to inhibit cooperative relations since others tend to feel less competent.

   a. True
   b. False

3. Knowledge power is found only in the upper management positions.

   a. True
   b. False

4. Managers with knowledge power use such knowledge solitarily so that it does not become "common" knowledge among all workers and the manager loses power.

   a. True
   b. False

5. Knowledge power is "born and not made."

   a. True
   b. False

6. Knowledge power can provide valid solutions to the vexing issues and problems facing the school district.

   a. True
   b. False

7. Punishment/coercive power has been found to foster long-term personnel performance in work activities.

   a. True
   b. False

8. Punishment power is used most often by first- and second-year managers.

   a. True
   b. False

9. Referent power is based on one's ability to delegate power to other employees.

   a. True
   b. False

10. Expert power is power that has been given a leader due to his or her position in the school system hierarchy.

    a. True
    b. False

11. Respect power is that which comes from the fact that the person is a "boss" in the system.

    a. True
    b. False

12. School principals, who give autonomy to teachers for making classroom decisions regarding parental problems, are demonstrating reward power.

    a. True
    b. False

13. A school principal who shows consideration to a teacher who is having problem with providing services for his or her special needs child is demonstrating transient power.

    a. True
    b. False

14. Leaders who demonstrate coercive power use recognition and other rewards to those that who performing in an excellent fashion in the classroom.

    a. True
    b. False

15. An employee who demonstrates special solutions to an organizational development problem that the school is facing is showing employee relationship power.

    a. True
    b. False

ANSWERS TO THE TRUE OR FALSE QUIZ

1. Answer to Question 1 is False. The person is demonstrating reward power.
2. Answer to Question 2 is False. Competency in knowledge generally leads to a feeling of respect on the part of coworkers.
3. Answer to Question 3 is False. Knowledge and information power can be held by both leaders and followers in the school setting. It is true that school leaders commonly have access to information that others in the system do not possess immediately. Nevertheless, a subordinate often is most knowledgeable in several aspects of human relations, student achievement, and other educational program matters.
4. Answer to Question 4 is False. Sharing of the best ideas for problem solution is a responsibility of school leaders. It is true, however, that giving solutions and having special knowledge that is "spread" among all members of the organization does lead to lesser personal power, but also can add to position, relationship, and referent power of the leader.
5. Answer to Question 5 is False. Knowledge and learning are ongoing, lifetime characteristics of effective individuals.

6. Answer to Question 6 is True. The ability to provide information that leads to the resolution of issues and problems facing the school is a prime example of knowledge power.
7. Answer to Question 7 is False. Although coercive power can bring about changes in an employee's negative behavior or performance, in the long run it can result in negative outcomes of resentment and decrease in employee loyalty.
8. Answer to Question 8 is False. There is no research evidence that punishment measures are associated with age or leadership tenure.
9. Answer to Question 9 is False. Referent power is influence that is gained by a leader due to a sense of loyalty, respect, admiration, friendship, or other positive characteristics on the part of his or her subordinates.
10. Answer to Question 10 is False. The characteristics set forth in the question describe position or legitimate power.
11. Answer to Question 11 is False. The so-called boss must earn loyalty and respect on the part of his or her subordinates or colleagues.
12. The answer to Question 12 is False. Position or legitimate power is being demonstrated in this entry. Giving autonomy to a teacher or telling him or her to just use his or her best judgment on parental matters demonstrates position power authority.
13. Answer to Question 13 is False. The principal is showing a caring attitude toward the teacher, which demonstrates relationship power.
14. Answer to Question 14 is False. Leaders who demonstrate coercive power use recognition and other rewards for those who are performing in an excellent fashion.
15. Answer to Question 15 is False. In this case, knowledge or expertise power is being demonstrated. However, such expertise and knowledge on the part of an employee can lead to improved human relationships and respect on the part of others.

POWER STRUCTURE ANALYSIS

Without much question, power analysis methodology, set forth by the authorities, Russell (1938), Hunter (1953), Dahl (1958), and McCarty and Ramsey (1971), has contributed most favorably to power theory and practices. Each of these authorities is discussed in the following section. Domhoff (1968) has contributed to the power structure literature by helping to define the work of the foregoing authorities and others.

The *events analysis approach,* utilized for identifying the community power structure, is attributed to Robert Dahl. The process is based on identifying the individuals in the community who have been directly involved in deciding the real issues facing the community. Party nominations, urban development, education reform, public bond issues, and election results may be issues chosen for identifying decision-making influentials. The key is to trace the specific people who were proactive in deciding the outcomes of these important decisions. The larger list of potential power influential is then best reduced by consensus. The problem, of course, is the question of whether or not one is really dealing with the individuals who made the decision.

The *reputational approach* involves going to persons in the center of community life and asking them to submit names of community influentials. Community agencies such as the director of the chamber of commerce, leading real estate broker in the community, and editor of the local newspaper. The number of names "collected" depends on the population of the school community. A consensus strategy is used commonly to reduce the number of persons on the list. The foregoing issues analysis procedure may be used to reduce the list additionally.

The two types of power most commonly identified in the literature are *collective power* and *distributive power*. Collective power is viewed as the ability of a group to achieve its goals and objectives. Thus, the group has the ability to sustain its operations in spite of the fact that other groups are not able to do so. Distributive power, on the other hand, focuses on the concept of who are the influentials that determine what is to be accomplished and what decisions will not reach the table. For example, an individual or group with distributive power possesses the means to decide if a school bond issue is to reach the status of being on a ballot for public consideration or perhaps getting a matter on the ballot that others could not otherwise do.

In a nutshell, community power individuals or groups have the power to determine what community issues are to be considered or not considered. In turn, their influence looms important in determining the outcomes of community decisions. Of special significance is the fact that persons in the power structure are influential in determining how the internal and external values and resources of the community are to be allocated. Just how many school districts are directly involved in the determination of the school community's power structure? Not many. However, all districts are faced with the decision outcomes that are being made and/or mandated by power authorities at the local, state, and federal levels.

TYPES OF POWER STRUCTURE

Four types of power structure are commonly recognized. McCarty and Ramsey (1967) noted that *monopolistic* (closed) power structure is more dominated and receives little opposition. The elite power structure is pyramidal in that the generals, captains, and lieutenants dominate the decision-making process in the community. There is little opposition. At the local school level, the superintendent of schools serves specifically to carry out the wishes of the power group. This fact does not mean that the school board is the power group, but it is quite possible that the school board is "ruled" by one member of the board. The voting on issues that are faced by the school board is always unanimous. School board members tend to be elected over and over again.

The *multiple-group* or pluralistic power structure is noncompetitive, conservative, and closed. This power structure is more democratic than the foregoing type, and voting is somewhat more "democratic" although there is considerable discussion before consensus is reached. In regard to the school board, the school superintendent commonly serves as a diplomat and professional advisor. Thus, he or she is well versed in the issues of the day and is able to participate in discussions related to the issues at hand.

The *competitive elite* or factional power structure is more diffused, and factional groups are constantly contending for their particular aims. The power structure tends to change depending on the issue or problem at hand. Thus, there is an ongoing struggle between groups and individuals to gain their preferred goals. Voting is seldom unanimous. Since issues are always changing, membership on the school board often changes. School board elections are always competitive, and new members tend to come on board quite frequently. Thus, school leaders must be flexible and able to work with the majority faction by using effective political strategies.

The *latent* power structure is generally inert but can come to life and be effective on issues for which it is especially interested. In general, however, the school superintendent is the individual who recommends what is needed, and the school board tends to support these actions. The school superintendent is the decision-maker. In such an inert environment, it tends to hold to the status quo. It could be said that the school board is not closely tied to community representation nor does it receive direct community support. The bottom line is the fact that the type of power structure that exists within the community most often is reflected in the school board as well.

The *segmented pluralistic* type of power structure is most open. Leadership specializes in different projects. It not only is most open but is also the most diffused. Leadership focuses on the issues/projects at hand. Discussion and voting are of importance for the purpose of reaching a group consensus. A unanimous vote commonly results in view of the group's efforts to reach an agreement. The leader or school superintendent generally serves as an advisor rather than simply carrying out the policies determined by the board. In this role, he or she is quite knowledgeable of the issues being faced and therefore actively participates in discussing the issues at hand. We note that the names given to the four common power structures tend to change from study to study.

It has been found empirically that influentials operate primarily on two levels. They are active on specific policy issues and on a personal base when their own children are involved in the outcomes of the decision. It was noted previously that school boards tend to reflect the same type of power structure as being practiced in the community. In addition, educators have been found to be most removed from public decision participation matters that often become their problems. Research has indicated that the general public is of the opinion that it cannot really reach the school administration and even if it does, their opinions are ignored. Therefore, special means must be taken to ensure the message is understood.

SUMMARIES OF THE FOUR TYPES OF POWER STRUCTURES WITHIN ORGANIZATIONS

1. Elite Monopolistic Power Structure (Dominated, Closed)

a. Receives little opposition in controlling the decision-making process.
b. Decisions are made by a core group of influentials.
c. School board is dominated by the power group; school superintendent is controlled with little administrative discretion.
d. School board generally turns to one member for decisions.
e. This power structure is pyramidal, if active control is absolute.
f. School board is selected on the assumption they will take advice from "leaders" outside the board mainly because they share the same ideology.
g. Board members receive little opposition and are reelected time and again.
h. Votes tend to be unanimous on all basic issues. One or two board members set the tone.
i. Power is derived from economics and the dominating political party.
j. School superintendent is primarily a functionary: (1) He or she tends to identify with the dominant interests and is in complete agreement with the major proposals of the school board; may give the impression of being inert. (2) School superintendent carries out policy rather than serving as a developer of policy. (3) School superintendent is chosen either unconsciously or deliberately who holds the beliefs of the power structure in place; follows the prevailing themes in the dominated community. (4) Business is done through the superintendent's office, but he or she is not a true decision-maker. This does not mean that the superintendent is not "effective" or doesn't like the role.

2. Competitive Elite or Factional Power Structure

   a. Leadership is specialized in different projects. Power group(s) act according to the issue or problem at hand. Decision-making commonly is revealed in two or more groups vying for power. Matters such as bond issues for school facilities, urban renewal, special needs programs, and others serve as the spark that ignites the specific power structure.

   b. This power structure is actually more open in that a factional school board usually reveals the importance of voting as opposed to discussion and consensus. If the vote is crucial, majority faction always wins. Factional boards depend on majority for decision success.

   c. School board members represent the viewpoint of one of the factions (e.g., labor vs. management, economic groups, political groups, occupations, religious groups).

   d. School board elections are "hotly" contested: one faction at one time, but balance changes as new members are elected.

   e. The school superintendent must work with the majority but becomes a political strategist since factions keep changing. In many instances, he or she serves as an arbitrator.

   f. The school superintendent needs to take a flexible stand on issues of a controversial nature allowing room to maneuver or retreat. Board members tend to see such behavior as "distrustful" which leaves the superintendent in an awkward position.

3. Segmented Pluralism (Pluralistic and Diffused; Most Open of the Four Power Types)

   a. Leadership is specialized in different projects. Power group acts according to the issue or problem at hand—bond issues, special needs program, new facilities, curriculum issues.

   b. School board members often represent particular interests, but there is no overall theme of power influence. Leadership varies according to the issues.

   c. Discussion prior to voting is of importance. Members are "equal" in status and treat each other as individuals where full discussion of problems and decisions by consensus is the name of the game. There is a consensus type of authority, and many poles of power are in evidence. The issue at hand is of concern; this leads to a "more open" operation.

   d. The school superintendent serves primarily as a professional advisor. He or she is not limited to carrying out policy only. The superintendent can approach the matter in a more statesman-like manner. Alternatives can be expressed and problems and consequences can be identified.

e. The school superintendent acts as a change agent and often presents proposals for various programs in the school system.

4. Inert Power Structure (Latent Behavior)

a. The school board is inactive and has no philosophical reinforcement from the community.
b. The school board neither represents nor receives reinforcement from the citizenry and thus tends to follow the recommendations of the superintendent and staff.
c. The school board acts to sanction the policies proposed by the superintendent, and although its right to approve or reject a matter is understood, the latent power structure tends to hold on to the status quo.
d. The school board looks to the superintendent for advice and shows a high degree of respect for the person in that position.
e. The school superintendent is the decision-maker who initiates action, and the school board approves it.
f. Because of the school board's inactivity, the school superintendent not only is free to act but must also do so if the program is to be effective.
g. The school board can "come alive" if the changes being offered are contrary to their desires. They will act to stop undesirable actions in such instances (e.g., reorganization of school districts).
h. The inert school power structure, according to research, is found most commonly in rural communities.

As previously noted in chapters 1 and 2, if the school superintendent is to understand and cope with the diverse demands and pressures that surround the office, he or she must understand the operation of power and influences in community decision-making. Once that this understanding is in place, the school superintendent is in a much better position to work with these power elements. Such understanding leads to a more effective utilization of professional energies and communication effectiveness.

RECOGNIZING AND ASSESSING THE CHANGES IN POWER STRUCTURE STATUS

The difficulty in distinguishing community members who are within the power structure is increased by ongoing shifts of power due to ongoing shifts in such things as elected leaders, economic health, population size, and societal norms. What are the signs that tend to indicate power changes for captains and/or generals formerly in the community power structure? There are several signs that can be tested or observed to help determine if one's current power influential is still in the "winners' circle." The five sign changes that follow are tell-tale factors.

Sign 1—Information source(s) becomes unreliable. Actual results that occur are contrary to the feed-in received. This suggests that the person is not on the inside anymore.

Sign 2—The individual doesn't want to be involved anymore. He or she states openly states that he or she "do[es] not want to be involved anymore. I've done my share so let others get involved for a while." Again, this suggests that the person no longer has access to the thinking and information of the current power structure.

Sign 3—Your power person goes public on community issues. This is commonly an indication that he or she has lost out regarding the inner power structure and now seeks support through general public backing.

Sign 4—Check population and business changes. Frequently, these matters bring changes in power structure due to new goals and conditions (e.g., age factors, mobility, economics, diversity).

Sign 5—Watch ongoing political party changes: who gets elected and who is associated with the winning party?

ROBERT DAHL AND FLOYD HUNTER: TWO MEMBERS OF THE POWER STRUCTURE RESEARCH HALL OF FAME

In the following section, two major studies of power structures, one by Robert Dahl and the other by Floyd Hunter, are discussed. Although both power studies are dated, each method looms important for its contributions to power structure research. Other studies that followed those by Dahl and Hunter most often reference these researchers and utilize methodologies contained in their original works. This is not to say that the studies by Dahl and Hunter have not received criticism concerning their basic assumptions and research methods; few, if any, early studies do not receive critical reviews by later researchers.

The criticisms center on several factors including the fact that the communities studied were not typical of other communities, times have changed and the data gathered do not reflect contemporary times, and the persons interviewed were inappropriate for truly identifying members of the power structure. In addition, critics contended that Dahl's model does not address the more serious issues of interest to the powerful. That is, Dahl failed to differentiate the real issues facing society; rather he dealt with issues that held little interest of the power captains in the community. Nevertheless, both studies give important clues to us for implementing power structure studies in local school-communities. This contention is illustrated by the local school power structure identification that is recommended for use by a school superintendent or other local school administrator presented later in this chapter.

In his study of politics in New Haven, Connecticut, Dahl used a technique of study that emphasized an analysis of a number of decisions in three issue areas: (1) party nominations, (2) urban development, and (3) public education. Persons representative of each issue area were asked to identify the most important decisions made in their area in recent years. Data about each decision were obtained by use of records, documents, newspapers, and numerous interviews. The interviews were conducted to determine patterns of personal involvement in the decisions identified. Then, a number of those persons in the decisions was interviewed.

The decisions selected for study in public education included: (1) selling the high schools to Yale and building two new ones; (2) accepting or rejecting a proposal to change procedures on promotions; (3) major appointments, including the appointment of an assistant superintendent for secondary education; (4) an eye-testing program; (5) a proposed ratio plan on salaries; (6) school budgets; (7) a proposal to deal with delinquency; (8) proposals to increase appropriations for school libraries.

A number of these decisions, especially numbers 2, 3, 4, and 7, appears to be professionally centered decisions. These decisions did not involve important questions of financial policy or fundamental innovations as was true with the other entries. In regard to number 1, the mayor and president of Yale University were central figures in a deal to sell the two schools for $3 million, a considerable amount of money at that time. Reportedly, by way of a process of shrewd fiscal and political maneuvering on the part of the mayor, which allowed the schools to be built on city-owned park property, the new high schools were built without a tax increase.

The promotion question, 3, appears to be of little concern. However, while the promotion of teachers to principalships faced little concern, it was reported that the question of appointing an assistant superintendent involved political bickering among the mayor, factions of the school board, the school superintendent, and the chairman of the Board of Education. In the final analysis, the mayor phoned the chair of the school board and told him whom he favored for the position. This power move appeared to resolve the issue, and the unanimous vote of the school board indicated as much. Nevertheless, the school superintendent had little to say about the appointment.

Unlike the education issues, Dahl's analysis found that public officials were firmly in control of decisions made in the urban redevelopment program. No other economic or social notables were noticeably involved in this issue. His study was notable in that he demonstrated that power in the city studied was pluralistic and not any one group could call the shots in this case of education. The multiple forces involved in the education decisions were not so involved in the city's urban redevelopment issue.

In a pluralistic power structure, an influential mayor can initiate but not necessarily command; he or she has to enter into the "bargaining" that takes place among a variety of interests.

Floyd Hunter's study of Regional City, as reported in his work, *Community Power Structure,* in 1953, represents an important turning point in the study of the decision-making process. In his reputational technique, persons at the center of community life are asked to nominate those leaders who, according to the informant's knowledge, are the most important leaders in the community.

Lists of leaders holding positions of prominence in business, government, and civic organizations and lists of wealthy and socially prominent persons are obtained from such sources as the chamber of commerce, League of Women Voters, local newspaper editors, civic club leaders, and other community agencies. The list of prominent persons is submitted to a cross-section of judges for the purpose of determining leadership rankings among those listed. Consequently, the study of power concentrates upon the presumed holders of power who are identified by the judges.

The final analysis of the procedure involves interviews with other persons in addition to the top leaders nominated by knowledgeable community members. This effort provides an opportunity to add the names of other persons to the list. Hunter found that the predominant power to decide questions of basic public policy was held, not by official policy-makers, but by persons who generally did not hold official positions. Power was wielded by informal structure of power elites. There was a great concentration of power among a few leaders drawn largely from the industrial, commercial, and financial interests of the city. These persons held a virtual monopoly over the major decisions being confronted.

Four levels of power structure were identified in a pyramidal structure as follows:

First rate: Industrial, commercial, financial owners, and top executives of large enterprises.

Second rate: Operational officials, bank vice presidents, public relations persons, small-business owners, top-ranking public officials, corporation attorneys, and major contractors.

Third rate: Civic organization personnel, civic agency board personnel, newspaper columnists, radio commentators, lower-level public officials, and selected organization executives.

Fourth rate: Professionals such as ministers, teachers, social workers, personnel directors, and other small-business managers, higher-paid accountants, and similar persons in financial accounting positions.

RECOMMENDED POWER STRUCTURE STRATEGIES
FOR SCHOOL SUPERINTENDENTS
AND OTHER EDUCATIONAL LEADERS

Norton (1968) noted that all too often a teacher, administrator, or other school worker takes lightly their responsibility for learning about the community. The "learning" procedure, in all too many instances, is a passive one and depends largely on incidental day-by-day personal activities and contacts. Therefore, he recommends getting to know the community in ten easy lessons. Norton asks the question, "Are you willing to take four hours to learn more about the school-community?" and then recommends ten easy ways for any school leader to get to know the school community. This is what he recommends:

(1) A new principal or central staff member should visit with the superintendent as well as selected members of the school board. The school board consists of members representative of several different aspects of the community. You'll gain some valuable information regarding the characteristics, customs, traditions, and politics of the community. In turn, the board members will be glad to know of your interest in this area of your work. You might explain your purpose for determining the school district's power structure and ask individual board members who might have been influential in their election or appointment to the office.

(2) Confer with the local manager of the chamber of commerce or locally prominent business person. These resources will have many contacts with the various "publics" of the community.

(3) Arrange to see the city manager or a city council person. Valuable insight into the public pulse can be gained through city officials. Will these city officials be too busy for such a conference? Why not call and find out? Don't let them keep you for more than 30 minutes.

(4) Visit with the president or director of the local Ministerial Association. The minister's role calls for a close association with the people of the community. This particular role provides this person with rather sensitive insights into community relations.

(5) Arrange to visit with the editor(s) of the local newspaper. Newspaper staffs are usually aware of the makeup of the community and are alert to the real community issues and concerns.

(6) Ask your secretary to arrange a meeting with your chief administrative assistants, including the business manager, head custodian, cafeteria manager, athletic director, and the secretary herself. Attempt to gain their viewpoints on the "publics" that they encounter in the fulfillment of their duties.

(7) Arrange to have morning coffee with one or more presidents of the local civic clubs. These persons are most likely prominent community leaders in their own right. Gain their ideas of the major issues being faced by the school community, and they can give you the names of other individuals who are involved in the various decisions being made on community issues.

(8) Ask the local parent-teacher association or council for 30 minutes of time at their next planning meeting. Emphasize your interest in gaining their views of the community and its educational views of purposes and objectives.

(9) Decide upon a teachers' group with whom you will visit about community relationships. There most likely is a logical teacher group or committee appropriate for your purposes. What about their assessments of community engagement in educational matters?

(10) While other publics, groups, agencies, and/or individuals in the community should be contacted, you already have enough information to provide valuable help in your work as a community leader. Spend time to reflect on your visits. How does the information gained in your visits help to answer foregoing questions relative to your needs to communicate with various groups and individuals in the school community? Who are the influentials in the community whose input you need in the decision-making process? How might you improve your communication with persons in the power structure of the community on an ongoing basis? What are the implications for your work as an educational leader in promoting and assuring quality education for the children and youth in your community?

Berkowitz and Schultz (2017) set forth one of the most informative and straightforward articles on involving key influentials in an initiative. Every school leader should have a copy of this article on his or her office desk. This article, which appears in *Community Tool Box,* states that influentials "are the people in your community whose opinions are respected, whose insights are valued, and whose support is almost always needed to make any big changes" (p. 1). They discuss several key points of major importance regarding the involvement of persons who are likely to know just where the power and influence within the community lies.

Personal contact is the crucial element at all stages of gaining the needed support. Influential people can be helpful in communicating with legislators and other supportive people in the community. It is of paramount importance that school personnel learn about the special interests of the influential person and understand what is important to them. In what ways have these persons been involved in various projects? How might the school leader appeal to the influential's personal interests and help them accomplish their goals? How will the accomplishment of the school district's initiative affect the business or interests and ideals of the influential person? How can that person be involved, and what steps need to be taken to gain such involvement?

It is of importance for the school personnel to give supporters the positive feedback in regard to their efforts. Make special note of how your educational project has served to improve the educational program and the learning culture of the school programs. Keep the influential aware of the positive results regardless of his or her actual involvement. Such positive feedback could serve to gain the influential's involvement in the future. Such follow-up can also be an indication of your sincere appreciation for their support of the initiative's success.

DATA ANALYSIS OF FEEDBACK RECEIVED FROM THE SERIES OF CONTACTS

The foregoing analysis of the feedback is communication of considerable importance. It serves to reduce the number of surprises that might otherwise be encountered. It serves to demonstrate your interest and concern for engaging the members of the community in the educational programs of the school. It opens the door to important communication and avoids the situations whereby you and your staff are talking only to yourselves. Just as airline pilots learn to cope with turbulence, the school leader must also make every attempt to live with normal turbulence by keeping abreast of community issues and keeping the school board knowledgeable about crises that are likely to occur. Be on top of community interests. By not doing so, the problem being faced most likely will have escalated beyond your ability to be most effective in its solution.

STEPS IN PLANNING AND DEVELOPING A POWER ANALYSIS FOLLOW-UP STRATEGY

Once a power analysis has been completed, then what? The following recommendations set forth several steps for determining a plan of action for utilizing the power structure information gained. Keep in mind that the personnel in the school district are not likely to have been directly involved in the implementation of the power structure analysis. Thus, a first task is that of creating an awareness of the need and benefits that can be gained with the new results of the school district's power structure data.

In sessions with the school superintendents and the chair of the school district's school board, take sufficient time to discuss the results of the power structure analysis and how his information will serve to achieve the purposes of the school district? To create an awareness of the need to utilize this information is of paramount importance. Discuss the roles that cabinet members must play and assign roles to the business, personnel, public relations, school facilities, and curriculum department heads.

Key are the questions: How do we utilize the wider power structure which we know now exists? What are the specific staff roles and priorities? How do we move at this time or move ahead of unexpected happenings? Take ample time to determine communication strategies. Establish a communication base and keep the base informed as to what activities are planned and the results of the plan that were implemented. Keep in mind that department heads and other staff personnel have other jobs to do. A more flexible staff structure might be needed in order to carry out the required tasks. School personnel, who are serving as political analyst, researchers, trouble shooters, public relations directors, and researchers, should be given serious consideration.

Each staff person has the task of helping the school superintendent and school board get outside the narrow realm of the school's internal operation. Unless the school personnel are sensitive to the social forces that permeate the school system, it will continue to be viewed as closed and perhaps dysfunctional. Communication with the school-community power structure will be instrumental in helping to see the system and the community as the influentials are viewing it. Such information is essential for knowing how to "turn on" the people and create a power structure to gain favor for the issue/problem/idea at hand.

There are no magic wands; school leadership cannot wait for someone or some other agency to define the school district's roles. Schools are in the middle of the political world and cannot hide this fact. School leaders need to know the answer to the question "who has the ear of the King?" School leaders must check themselves on two basic political rules: (1) Count your votes and (2) then count them again!

As stated by Herrity (2010), "The era of change in our communities is accelerating rapidly due to the dramatic increase of power groups operating inside the local community. These power groups are seeking and desiring an improved quality of life for themselves and others. Future gains or rewards are determined by the nature of your interaction with the power network. As a community member and advocate who supports improved lifestyles, it is highly desirable to possess the skills necessary to be successful with community power actors. Such skills are needed in order to minimize potential conflicts and maximize access to valuable resources" (p. 2).

A LOOK AT LOCAL SCHOOL POLITICS:
A CASE IN POINT

Political issues and problems within the local school-community school board are commonly heating up school board races and conflicting thinking among and between the school boards and voices of parents and school personnel. A recent case in point is the matter of *political indoctrination* explained by Miguel Otarola of the *Star Tribune* of Minneapolis, Minnesota (2017, October 14). We describe this political conflict from the report presented by Otarola.

The heated argument was initiated, according to Otarola, by an article that was published in a magazine, *Thinking Minnesota,* that was sent to all households in Edina, Minnesota. Reportedly, its author said that an effort to teach radical equity and "indoctrinate" students in "left-wing political orthodoxies" has threatened the district's quality education. Parents and school board candidates reacted to the article, and it became the major focus on a school board candidate forum; 12 candidates were vying for four school board seats, a majority of the board.

Both positive and negative voices were posted on Facebook; the topics of diversity, equity, globalization, race, student rights, and other concerns were matters of discussion. Criticisms of what was termed the article's misleading falsehoods were expressed by some persons. Other persons viewed the article as a political attempt to influence the forthcoming school board election. The Center of the American Experiment, that published the article, was accused of politicking to influence the forthcoming board election. However, the Center president stated, "We don't do politics, we do policy." Some persons expressed the thought that it was important for board candidates to discuss political ideologies in schools; others set forth the opinion that "we need to depoliticize the schools and create an environment of openness." There appeared to be a general feeling that community members would definitely pay attention to the upcoming school board race.

LOCAL SCHOOL POWER STRUCTURE ISSUES
AND POSITIVE RESULTS

Most everyone can remember a time when a school issue became highly controversial and politically connected. Even when the recommendation is viewed as being in the best interests of the students, it can be viewed as being politically based by the persons that it effects. In this case, a dated elementary school was labeled as unsafe. Its wooden floors were "contaminated" with floor oils that were used in sweeping them, and the electrical components within the school were viewed as being outdated and dangerous. Engineers had recommended that the school be condemned.

In a meeting with parents of the school community, the engineer's recommendations were reviewed and parents were told of the plans to have their children attend a different neighborhood school that would require new classroom additions. Fillips School was located inside the city on approximately one acre of land. The Hawthorn School, that the students would attend, was located on a ten-acre site. Nevertheless, the parents attending the information session were unimpressed with the school board's recommendation. After all, the Fillips Elementary School was a "landmark" in the city of Anilas.

One critical parent attending the session stood and suggested that the move was a political one in an attempt to hire a local contractor to do the construction for the additional classrooms needed at the Hawthorne School. The owner of the construction company just happened to be a good friend of the school board president. "Why can't you just build a new school on the same Fillips School site?" asked another parent. The question was answered by the fact that the Fillips' site was only one acre; modern elementary schools need at least ten acres. In addition, it was pointed out that Fillips had little or no playground space and Hawthorne had space for a tennis court, baseball diamond, and a large grass area for school games and other ceremonies. The parent responded that they won't let the children play on the Fillips School area anyway.

False rumors ran abundant. "The Anilas city mayor has his eyes on the Fillips School site for a new computer store that he was planning to open." "The school superintendent did not like the fact that Fillips School did not do well on the required academic tests required by the school board and this was one way to get the school principal out of his administrative role." "The new assistant school superintendent does not like the small neighborhood school philosophy established by the school board many years ago." Ultimately, the city placed a condemned sign on the Fillips School and the school was shut down and demolished.

The students entered Hawthorne Elementary School the next year with no issues or problems. The city mayor did not build a store on the Fillips site. Hawthorne students' test scores increased, and the school district's assistant superintendent was promoted to the position of superintendent upon the retirement of the former school superintendent. During this interim period, a bond issue was initiated for the addition to the Hawthorne Elementary School, a new gymnasium for one of the district's junior high schools, a new athletic field at one high school, and maintenance repairs at several other elementary school sites. This information is noted due to the fact that one of the school district's primary influentials was asked to serve as chair of the bond issue promotion committee. Without question, this positive political move served most favorably and resulted in promoting the approval of the bond issue for the Anilas school district.

Take a moment to consider the implications of the two foregoing stories. What primary points were the stories trying to underscore in relation to the chapter purposes? For example, how does each story give some clues to the identification of power structure at the local school level? What might the stories reveal concerning the nature of issues and problems that are faced and the involvement of various power influences at the local school level? What content in the stories conjures up thoughts about power structure communication?

STRENGTHENING LOCAL SCHOOL POWER BY IMPROVING ORGANIZATIONAL DEVELOPMENT ACTIVITIES

Thus far, an emphasis has been placed on determining external sources that can empower the schools' ability to achieve its important educational goals and objectives. This importance is the basic message of this book. Nevertheless, self-improvement internally of educational policy and administrative practices is a factor of paramount importance. Ineffective school board practices and ineffective administrative leadership would most likely remain in practice even if it were possible for school personnel to determine community power structure information. Without effective internal organizational development, just knowing the power elites would not be productive.

The following section focuses on improving internal organizational development at the local school district level, and in doing so, improving the power bases of the local school district. We ask the question, "What is the most important responsibility of the local school board?" Some persons would argue that hiring the school superintendent is the board's most important job. Without question, hiring an effective school superintendent is of paramount importance. However, we submit that developing viable education school policy that sets forth the educational ends to be achieved is the number 1 responsibility of a local school board. Effective educational administration follows closely behind guiding policy development.

A CASE IN POINT

The importance of the foregoing discussion relative to organizational development and "getting the house in order" is illustrated by a current internal problem between the school board, school superintendent, and the school district's education association. The article reporting the situation appeared in a leading city newspaper with the title *Teachers:* ' "No Confidence" in District Leaders.' In this case, the teachers' union issued a rare vote of "no confidence" against the school district's leadership.

The related "problems" of this case are beyond the scope of this chapter. However, the school superintendent reportedly commented that "we find ourselves being bullied online, cyberattacks, personal attacks, harassment of a district that is truly focused on our students, on our employees . . . and meanwhile, we have a media that has been promoting stories that have very little merit. One might even define it as "fake news." Reference was made to "politically motivated individuals who like to shift the focus of the school district away from accountability and learning."

The president of the state's education association commented, "For the teachers and staff to weigh in at such a high rate, they must feel almost no trust or confidence that work climate will improve." The point is this: How might a prior political analysis have served to eliminate or alleviate the negative outcomes of this situation?

KNOWLEDGE QUIZ ON THE TOPICS OF POLICY DEVELOPMENT AND ORGANIZATIONAL DEVELOPMENT

Directions: Check the best answer for each question posed. Do not just guess the answer; rather just skip that question and move onto the next. Then check your responses with the correct answers at the end of the quiz.

1. Which response best defines the term *policy*?

    a. a statement that answers the question of how a procedure is to be administered.
    b. a law that is the result of a legislative bill passed by the state legislature.
    c. a statement as to how the school board will implement its responsibilities.
    d. a rule set forth by any local school that governs the conduct of teachers and students.
    e. a statement that centers on the aims of the school district's purposes and answers the question of what to do.

2. School district policies can be adopted only by:

    a. the school board.
    b. the school superintendent.

c. official actions of the school superintendent and school board.

d. final authorization of the state board of education.

e. none of the above.

3. The statement "There will be no smoking in at any time in the buildings or on school district property" is a(n):

   a. school rule.
   b. school policy.
   c. administrative regulation.
   d. state law.

4. The statement "Standardized testing in the subject areas of English, mathematics, and science will be administered in the last month of school for all students completing grade eight and are to be administered by the school guidance counselor of each school" is a(n):

   a. school policy.
   b. school district policy.
   c. administrative regulation.
   d. none of the above.

5. The term *organizational development* is commonly defined as:

   a. staff development.
   b. the study of organizational change and performance.
   c. people helping each other to unleash the human spirit and human capability in the workplace.
   d. the movement of an organization from its current state to some future and hopefully more effective state.
   e. an effort to improve the effectiveness of all components of an organization using the knowledge of behavioral science.

6. Check each entry below that is an activity or term associated with organizational development.

   a. decision engineering.
   b. knowledge management.
   c. organizational communication.
   d. organizational diagnosis.
   e. collaboration.
   f. value network.
   g. social network.
   h. action research.
   i. assister and resister analysis.
   j. communications networks.

7. The terms *Delphi Technique, Nominal Group Technique, PERT,* and *Systems Analysis* are:

   a. primarily related to planning and decision-making strategies.
   b. strategies for determining community power structure(s).
   c. strictly action research terms for determining program effectiveness.
   d. terms related to the scientific management era and school efficiency.
   e. organizational development terms that entered the education process in the early twenty-first century.

8. Power structure analysis relates to the concept of organizational development since:

   a. both concepts focus on the development and implementation of policies and regulations that serve to facilitate the improvement of education goals and objectives.
   b. both concepts are based on democratic principles.
   c. both concepts are void of political intentions.
   d. are non-controversial.
   e. none of the above.

9. The primary purpose of relating power structure analysis to the processes of organizational development is to:

   a. underscore the need for local schools and school districts to be sufficiently prepared to utilize the information gained by having effective school governance activities in place.
   b. demonstrate what is meant by action research.
   c. demonstrate to the school community that you have an open system.
   d. underscore the importance of organization development.
   e. none of the above.

10. Organizational development has which of the following characteristics?

   a. The primary, although not exclusive, goal is to improve organizational effectiveness.
   b. Focuses on change within the entire organization, including departments, work groups, and individuals within the organization.
   c. Is a planned and long-range strategy for managing change while also recognizing that the dynamic environment requires the ability to change quickly to changing circumstances.
   d. It recognizes the need for planned follow-up to maintain changes that inevitably occur.
   e. It involves planned interventions and requires skills in working with internal and external individuals and groups, and whole organizations.
   f. None of the above.
   g. All of the above.

SUMMARY OF ANSWERS TO THE KNOWLEDGE-QUIZ

1. The answer to Question 1 is "e," a statement that centers on the aims of the school district and answers the question of what to do. Policies are: (1) assertions of the goals of the school system, (2) general statements related to an area of major importance to the citizenry and leave room for discretionary judgment by the school superintendent and professional staff, (3) the major concern of the school board; only the school board can adopt school policy, (4) applicable for long periods of time.
2. The answer to Question 2, "school district policies can be adopted only by the school board" is, "a." It is true that state legislatures and the courts often require the direction for what the school district must implement. In such cases these "mandates" are viewed as policies even though they commonly do not follow the general form of a policy as defined in this chapter.

   For example, such policies often include the procedures necessary for implementing the policy and, therefore, set forth certain administrative regulations as well.
3. The answer to Question 3, "there will be no smoking at any time in any of the buildings on school property," is "c," an administrative regulation. The statement is specific and leaves no room for administrative discretion. It sets forth the time that smoking is not allowed, sites of the no-smoking restrictions. In regard to smoking, the statement tells how one must behave.
4. The answer to Question 4, "standardized testing in the subject areas of English, mathematics, and science will be administered in the last month of school for all students completing grade eight and will be administered by the guidance counselor of each school," is "c." The statement is specific and leaves no room for discretion. It specifies just what subjects will be tested, when they will be tested, which students will take the tests, and who is assigned to administer the tests.
5. The answer to Question 5, "the theory, organizational development, is commonly defined as," is all letters "b" through "e." Each of these definitions is appropriate for the purposes of effective organizational development. Although the term *staff development* is a part of organizational development, it is not as all-inclusive as the other entries.
6. The answer to Question 6, "check each term that is associated with organizational development," is "j." Each term is defined as follows:

   Decision engineering is a framework that unifies a number of best practices for organizing decision making.
   Knowledge management is the way in which organizational leader takes special means for keeping abreast of new research and best practice information for application in the practices of the organization.
   Organizational communication refers to the channels of communication among and between members of the school or school system.

Collaboration is the practice of purposely arranging for opportunities for individuals and groups to meet and discuss activities, methods, successes, and needs related to their work.

Value network is a business analysis network that describes special and technical resources within and between businesses.

Social network analysis uses network and graphic theories to investigate social structures within the school community.

Action research is the research administered by one or more teachers in the classroom setting for evaluating and assessing the results of an activity or method of instruction.

Assister & resister Analysis differs in that assister analysis serves to suggest ways to minimize resistance and to learn of the reasons why objections are occurring. *Resister analysis* focuses on determining the reasons why the proposal/change is being challenged.

Communication networks are those media and human sources of internal and external information channels that are used to receive and deliver information of importance to the effective operations of schools and school districts.

7. The answer to Question 7, "the Delphi Technique, Nominal Group Technique, PERT, and systems analysis," is "a," primarily related to planning and decision-making strategies. For example, PERT, a program evaluation review technique, requires networking planners to make close time estimates for the completion of each job and activity. Time estimating is of great importance because it helps to keep a project moving along a reasonable timeline and allows those involved to know where they are in relation to where they should be for completing the project. A listing of steps in a PERT procedure is set forth in table 3.1. Following table 3.1, is figure 3.1, which illustrates a PERT network in operation.

Table 3.1   PERT Procedure

Steps
1. Project goal is determined.
2. Set forth the primary objectives to be achieved.
3. Develop/brainstorm project activities chart.
4. Evaluate and assess the relationships and dependencies of the primary objectives.
5. Develop communication, social, and value networks.
7. Evaluate and assess logic of networks.
8. Set forth estimations of time demands.
9. Identify critical path of work activities.

10. Re-assess time allocations and progress information.
11. Re-adjust project activity chart as revealed by progress information.
12. Evaluate completion time with progress activities and consider improvements in terms of plusses and minuses of work activities utilized.

Sample PERT Network

A PERT sample network is shown in figure 3.1. In this sample, collaborative teams 1, 2, and 3 initiate specific design tasks that are coordinated by and completed according to agreed-upon target dates. Each design task team sends its results to a program task team, once again according to a planned completion target date. Each program task team must complete its program task before the merger task can forward its merging task results to number 5 for testing. Depending on the test results and when results are shown to meet expectations, the project ends and is implemented according to plans set forth.

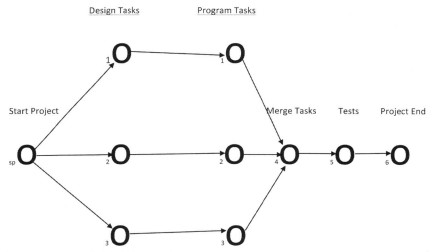

Figure 3.1. Sample PERT Network

The answer to Question 8, "power structure analysis relates to the concept of organizational development since," is "a," both concepts focus on the development of policy and regulation that serve to facilitate the improvement of educational goals and objectives.

9. The answer to Question 9, "the primary purpose of relating power structure analysis to the processes of organizational development," is "a," to be sufficiently prepared to utilize information gained by having effective school

governance activities in place. Unless the school board and administrative staff are prepared sufficiently to evaluate and assess information gained from informative sources in the school community, efforts to identify the power structure will be utilized in vain. The primary intention of power structure is to determine those human resources that need to receive the importance of ongoing school issues and to gain their feedback relative to their opinions relative to the issues, problems, and policies being proposed.

10. The answer to Question 10, "organizational development has which of the following characteristics?," is "g," all of them. Each entry identifies a characteristic of the organizational development (OD) concept. Keep in mind that OD looms important for establishing an effective internal school system. Without this assurance, power structure analysis will fall short of its purposes.

KEY CHAPTER IDEAS AND RECOMMENDATIONS

- The operations of power structure influences within the school community must be identified if school leaders are to manage the diverse demands and pressure that are bound to be present.
- Power structure analysis serves to develop an understanding of how influentials go about exercising their power and to find out the kinds of issues, problems, and situations in which the power is utilized.
- Empirical evidence tends to support the fact that school board members are not fully aware of the importance of being knowledgeable and skilled in the political arena.
- Power structure is defined in many ways, but commonly constitutes those persons and groups in the nation, city, or organization who constitute the actual ruling power relative to what is to be done and what is not to be done.
- The early work of Dahl and Hunter, among others, served to provide guidance for school leaders to identify the school district's power structure. These findings should be recommended study in school board in-service sessions and in administrative preparations programs in higher education.
- Four types of power structures commonly are found in school communities: elite, competitive, segmented, and inert. Each of these types holds implications for the ways in which school leaders go about their administrative responsibilities.

- The ways in which the school board and school leaders can identify power structure have been recommended and should be implemented by school leaders and school boards to gain ways and means for gaining support for important policies and financial support for educational purposes.
- Organizational development (OD) looms important for being able to apply power structure feedback. OD principles and procedures should be included in administrative programs in higher education and in in-service sessions for school board members.
- Internal policy and administrative regulation effectiveness will receive a higher level of community support if effective power structure analysis is implemented and utilized by school leaders.

DISCUSSION QUESTIONS

1. Assume that you are the school superintendent and a closed session of the school board is being held. The session was set to discuss personnel matters, and the matter of the resistance to the proposed school bond issue came to the floor. Rather than discuss this topic in the closed session, you were asked to draft a proposal regarding the bond issue concerns and present the school board. Take time to outline your response on the issue keeping in mind the information set forth in this chapter.
2. In your present school district or one in which you are most familiar, what is your assessment of the school district's knowledge of the community's power structure on a scale of 1 low to 5 high? Then, give thought to how this knowledge might be advantageous or disadvantages to the school district's program purposes.
3. What is meant by the contention that a school district's power structure strategy is dependent on many factors, including the status of the organizational development within the school district?
4. Assume that, as school superintendent, you were able to schedule a meeting with a person who had been known as a community influential. List three questions that you would likely ask him or her.
5. Internal awareness of the importance of school politics and power structure is viewed as being of paramount importance in this chapter. If possible, open the question of educational politics in a group of professionals in your school district or in some other setting which you might suggest. What purpose questions relative to the discussion might you recommend and why?

Case Study 3.1   We Accept Your Plans to Give Teachers the Authority That They Deserve

Hawthorne School District
Hawthorne, Lafayette
Office of Lafayette Teachers Association

"Teachers Leading the Way"
To: Dr. Dylan Joseph, Supt.
From: Tyler Scott, President, LTA
Re: Respecting Teacher Authority
Date: April 20

Your recent address to the Hawthorne School District professional teachers group was much appreciated and taken to heart. We, too, will appreciate your several recommendations for improving the authority of Hawthorne teachers and their inclusion in the school district's decision-making process. We applaud this opportunity to recognize the professional talents within the teaching personnel. Your statement of recognizing a teacher's autonomy in the classroom was received with much agreement.

In order to address your thoughts on this matter, the officers of the teachers' association want to express their dissatisfaction with several present conditions and activities and are suggesting new and different approaches to several of them. One priority change that we want to see in place ties to your authority view of teacher talents. Policy development, in most every case, holds implications for the work of the professional teacher. Therefore, we ask that one member of the teachers' association be appointed to sit with the school board in order to give input on policies discussed and approved at school board meetings. Our teacher would not have voting privileges.

Secondly, our association members have been concerned about the current negotiation procedures that have resulted in a win-lose process. Quid pro quo approaches tend to favor the school board and leave teachers at a great disadvantage. We want to assume a win-win approach whereby teachers are able to apply the authority that you suggested in your speech last month. We would like to recommend that our negotiation requests be submitted under the headings of first priority, second priority, and highly desirable. That is, first priority request should be viewed as "fair and reasonable" as you pointed out as one of our teachers' characteristics.

We ask that your office take the leadership on these recommendations and ask that you present them, along with me, to the school board at the next board meeting. We need to hear from you immediately, since our recommendations reflect the ideas set forth in your wonderful speech. Your support is appreciated. "It's not too late, to cooperate."

QUESTIONS

1. Case 3.1 parallels an actual situation in a real school district. Of course, names have been changed, and some details have been altered so as not to pose problems, but to make the case more challenging. Assume the role of Superintendent Joseph and set forth administrative procedures that would be implemented in response to the memo sent by the president of the teacher's association. With whom might you confer on this matter?

   What additional information might you seek? Would you contact the school board members at this time? Why or why not? You're the school superintendent. Your speech, apparently, motivated the teachers' association response. What are you going to do?

REFERENCES

Bal, V., Campbell, M., Steed, J., & Meddings, K. (2008). *The role of power in effective leadership.* AACCL Research White Paper. Center for Creative Leadership.

Berkowitz, B., & Schultz, J. (2017). Involving key influentials in the initiative. *Community Tool Box.* Center for Community Health and Development. Lawrence, KS: University of Kansas.

Berlet, C. (1968–2014). *Introduction to power structure research.* Research for Progress (blogsite). From the web: http://www.researchforprogress.us/topic/39042/power-structure-research/.

Burris, V. (2012). *Who rules? An internet guide to power structure Research.* Eugene, OR: University of Oregon.

Cambridge Advanced Learner's Dictionary (4th ed.) (2018). Cambridge, England: University of Cambridge Press.

Dahl, R. A. (1958). A critique of the ruling elite model. *American Political Science Review.* New Haven, CT: Yale University Press.

Domhoff, G. W. (1968). The power elite & its critics. In G. W. Domhoff & H. B. Ballard (Eds.). *C. Wright Mills and the Power Elite,* pp. 251–258. Boston, MA: Beacon Press.

Domhoff, G. W. (2005a). The basics of studying power. (webpage). *Who Rules America.* Santa Cruz, CA: University at Santa Cruz. On the web: https://whorulesamerica.ucsc.edu/methods/studying_power.html.

Domhoff, G. W. (2005b). Power structure research and the hope for democracy. (webpage). *Who Rules America.* Santa Cruz, CA: University at Santa Cruz. On the web: https://whorulesamerica.ucsc.edu/methods/power_structure_research.htmlSanta Cruz.

Herrity, J. P. (2010). *Understanding community power structures.* Consulting Solutions for Organizations. West Des Moines, IA: Preferred Visions.

Hunter, L. (1953). *Company power structure.* Chapel Hill: University of North Carolina Press.

Kelman, H. (1958). Compliance, identification, and internalization: Three processes of attitude change. *Journal of Conflict,* 2, 51–60.

McCarty, D. J., & Ramsey, C. E. (1971). The school managers: Power and conflict in American public education. Westport, CT: Greenwood Publishing Corporation.

Merriam Webster (2017, December 19). Elitist power group. *ESTABLISHMENT.*

Morgan, G. (1986). *Images of organization.* Newbury Park, CA: Sage.

Norton, M. S. (1968, September). Know your community in ten easy lessons. *The Clearing House,* 1. v. 13. Teaneck, NJ: Fairleigh Dickinson University.

Otarola, M. (2017). *Change of "political indoctrination" heats up Edina school board race.* From the web: http://wwwstartribune.com/miguel-otarola/396828811/

Russel. B. (1938). *A new social analysis.* New York, NY: Routledge.

Wikepedia (2018, January 8) Power (Social and Political). On the web: https://en.wikipedia.org/wiki/Power_(social_and_political)

Chapter 4

Improving the Ability
to Understand and Participate
in the Political World of Education

Primary chapter goal: To discuss the ways in which education leaders can increase their knowledge of politics and become more effective participants in their political world and to stress the need for much-improved research relative to promoting new innovations for educational reform that would affect the political influence of education in a positive manner.

"Influential people can provide an immense boost to the work we do in improving our communities. . . . By understanding who they are and how to include them in our efforts, we greatly improve the chances that our work will succeed. And that puts us on the road to becoming influential people ourselves—the kind people come to when they want to get things done" (Berkowitz & Schultz, 2017, p. 8). These authors set forth a reality goal for school leaders. As is true in the case of any program of personal improvement, a planned effort for improving one's political savvy is a realistic goal for school leaders.

This chapter centers on how potential and current leaders can work to become more qualified in procedures for identifying community power structures, being more effective in the world of politics of which education is a part and recommending strategies and programs for effective participation in school-community political activities. In a study by Shelton in 1989, she found that many school superintendents did not feel compelled or even at all comfortable with a change in their role as political lobbyist for their district. In fact, superintendents did not view such an activity as something that they should be doing. This fact is part of the problem, and this thinking continues to exist among educators three decades later.

Gareth Morgan (1986), in his seminal book on images of education, points out clearly that organizations are political systems, and as such, systems of government, schools, and school systems vary according to the political principles employed. As Morgan contends, "By attempting to understand organizations as systems of government, and by attempting to unravel the detailed politics of organizational life, we are able to grasp important qualities of organization that are often glossed over or ignored" (p. 143).

We are of the opinion that superintendents today have reserved opinions relative to political participation. There are several reasons for the continuing belief that political involvement is outside their concern. First, and perhaps foremost, is the fact that school superintendents are ill-prepared to assume such a political role. In addition, they do not appear to see the state and federal politics within their job description or are too busy with other issues and problems within their school districts to get involved with the "external" politics at the state and federal levels. It is true that educators should stay clear of the world of "dirty politics." We contend that the fear of losing state and/or federal financial support is another reason for the non-involvement of school leaders in the political issues and problems that they believe will affect their ability to achieve school goals and objectives.

We have noted in previous chapters of this book that superintendents and school boards have lessened their local decision-making control by purchasing their policies and regulations from the state school board associations. This practice has to stop. School board associations should attend to their role as a resource for providing instructional services for understanding the strategies of policy and regulation development and leave the actual local school policy development to local school authorities.

School board members and school superintendents must come to grips with the fact that times have changed, and they must become more knowledgeable and active in the external political environment in which the school is a part or be left behind as policy leaders for the education of children and youth. In an early study by Grady and Bryant (1991), the research results argued for administrative preparation and professional development programs that better reflect the real world, the world of politics.

The status of educators as political leaders was judged as being "unqualified" by most authorities in the early 1970s. As stated by Turner (1970), "Unfortunately, few educators are qualified to function in the political domain. Therefore, it is likely that special consultants or new positions will [be] needed to provide the technical expertise necessary for such activity" (p. 43). Nearly fifty years later, this contention still remains valid.

For school leaders to fulfill the educational goals that commonly are expressed in their mission and vision statements, they must have the freedom to express the "state of school affairs" in their school districts and play an active role, not only in local school-community affairs, but in the political arena of the local community and state. This means that school personnel must be knowledgeable and willing to communicate openly, positively, and confidently with the school district's educational circumstances and do so without the fear of financial loss of state and/or federal funding. In addition, state administrator associations must have the freedom to participate in the political arena of the state without the loss of being tax exempt.

A BIT OF HUMOR

The Fighting Tigers football team was losing the game in the third quarter by a score of 24 to 0. The opposing Bulldogs football players were big, rough, and ready. Their big line players were blitzing and the smaller Tiger backfield players were being "hit hard" on every play; two of their backfield players already were out with injuries. After a first down play by the Tigers that resulted in a 5-yard loss, Coach Smith called out to the quarterback, "Give the ball to Calhoon!" But, Jenkins carried the ball on the next play for another 5-yeard loss. Once again, Coach Smith called out, "I said, give the ball to Calhoon, give the ball to Calhoon!!" The quarterback yelled back, "Calhoon don't want the ball!"

Involvement in competitive politics can be troublesome, and some leaders do not want to carry this responsibility. They commonly argue that education should not be included in politics. One school superintendent commented that he was not interested in dealing with the ugly field of politics and went on to comment that he would recommend what was needed educationally or what should be done and it was the responsibility of the citizenry to decide if it wanted to get things done or not. Perhaps the attitude was a personal way out, but not realistic or productive. This kind of "naiveté" gives the individual a personal reason for his or her non-involvement, but really demonstrates a lack of courage and understanding.

POLITICS AND PREPARATION PROGRAMS: A SINE QUA NON OF CHANGE

As is the case with gaining any knowledge and skill, learning is essential. How and where does one gain skill in dealing with politics? In the case of educational administration, course work in the politics of education is sparse in educational administration preparation programs. As stated by Bottoms and O'Neill (2001), "Before we can redesign schools, we must redesign the programs that prepare school leaders" (p. 5). However, such course work is available in some quality institutions. For example, the Ohio State University offers a 3-credit course, School-Community Relations and Politics, in their 30–33 semester-hour Masters of Arts program in educational administration.

One course only is limited at best, but there are other activities that higher education programs could offer for school administrators.

Such an on/off campus course might be offered in administrative preparation programs whereby students are able to witness: (1) explanations of the dynamics of current education debates in references to the long-standing tensions among the different purposes of schooling, (2) explanations of the outcomes of said debates through important models of political action and policymaking, (3) the assumptions that lie behind current reform ideas, and (4) actual political debates and then discuss the relationships between state policymaking and party politics. Such preparatory experiences hold considerable potential for students preparing for administrative roles in education.

MODEL COURSE OF PROFESSOR REBECCA JACOBSEN: POLITICS AND EDUCATION

Michigan State University offers a course, politics and education, that focuses on the forces that shape education policy, with an emphasis on governmental structures, stakeholders, public engagement, and current policy issues and political contexts. The focus of the course is set forth in the following section of the chapter. The university course outline is presented as an excellent example of one course offered in higher education to inform students of the political world of education policy. Due to the importance of such courses for educational administration leaders, we gained the permission of the instructor, Professor Rebecca Jacobsen, to include the following course syllabus in this chapter.

EAD 943: Politics and Education
Spring 2017, Room 133E Erickson Hall
Mondays from 12:40–3:30 PM
Michigan State University

Professor Rebecca Jacobsen
201C Erickson Hall
517–353–1993
rjacobs@msu.edu (This is the best way to reach me.)
Office Hours: By appointment. Just email me and we will set up a time.

Course Description

This course is an introduction to the complex and often contested field of politics and education. The purpose of the course is to provide students with an understanding of the forces that shape educational policy, with an emphasis on governance structures, stakeholders, public engagement, and current policy issues and political contexts.

It begins with an overview of the development of politics and education as a field. We then examine major theories of policy making which will serve as a guide for understanding who gets what, when and how as we examine different education policy issues. The course provides opportunities to apply theoretical perspectives to "mini" case studies of education policymaking processes in organizational settings of particular interest to students.

Focus of the Course

Harold Lasswell, American political scientist and professor of law at Yale University said, *"Politics is who gets what, when, and how."* This will be our guiding big idea throughout the course. Who is able to get what from the education system? Who is able to get what from education policy leaders? When are different groups able to get particular policies passed? How are they able to have influence?

To examine these questions, we will focus on the US school system. Comparisons to other political systems are welcome. Further, we will consider:

The Policy-Making Process

- How is policy made in education?

  - What issues become policy problems? How and why?
  - How do politics shape implementation of good ideas?
  - What role does research and evidence play in shaping the policy-making process?

- Who gets a say in policy making?
- What theories explain why some policies are adopted while other policy ideas go unexamined?

Changing Power Dynamics and Governing Public Education

- Who has been influential in deciding education policy?

  - Who has formal power?
  - Who has informal power?

- How has this above list changed and shifted overtime?
- What are the advantages/disadvantages to alternative governance arrangements?

- What venues do different groups/individuals use to shape education policy?
- What strategies do different groups/individuals use to shape education policy?

Course Requirements

1) Readings, Class Participation, and Attendance

Learning how to think and talk critically about ideas and evidence are central tasks for the advanced graduate student. Accordingly, it is very important that all members of the class do the required reading and do so *before* the class session at which it will be discussed. It is expected that students will bring questions related to the text to each class and make references to the reading during class discussions.

Regular on-time attendance and full participation in class is critical to learning. Of course, illness and other emergencies cannot be avoided (within reason). If you are unable to attend a class session, you must email me in advance. If you miss more than one class, additional work will be expected to make up for the missed class sessions. Decisions for what is considered appropriate make up work will be dealt with on a case-by-case basis. Students are responsible for initiating this process.

I take class participation seriously. That means having things to say (and questions to ask) that are interesting, original, and helpful to the other students. It also means listening to others and building upon their ideas. I expect all students to contribute to the discussion in a manner that is respectful and thoughtful. The professor reserves the right to adjust your grade as a response to absences or excessive tardiness.

How to Read

I know, I know. We all know *how* to read. But reading effectively for a doctoral course is a different style of reading. To prepare for class, I HIGHLY recommend you bring the following notes to each class.

1. Getting the Basics Down (You DON'T need to know every single idea in every single article!):
   a. What is the **argument** of the piece? (1 sentence)
   b. What **evidence/method** did the piece use to support the argument? (list)
   c. Who is (are) the author(s) **responding** to? (2–4 sentences)

      i. Are they building on an existing argument?
      ii. Are they challenging an existing argument?

iii. Are they elaborating/refining an argument?

iv. Are they incorporating other disciplinary ideas (outside of more typical education frameworks)?

d. How does the piece **contribute** to the field's understanding of the issues? (1–3 sentences)

e. How **effective** is the argument and evidence in your opinion? (3–5 sentences)

i. What assumptions does (do) the author(s) make?

ii. What's missing from the analysis?

iii. Do you know of existing counter evidence?

iv. Is the study generalizable?

v. Do you think there is a "real world" application for the ideas in the piece?

2. Connecting to the Class Session:

a. Step back and ask: What does this reading contribute to the session topic identified on the syllabus? How do the readings for the week agree/disagree? What's the root of the disagreement?

3. Connecting to the Course:

a. Step back again and ask: How does the reading address the big ideas of the course? How does the reading contribute to our understanding of the politics and education?

4. What's Next:

a. If you were to take up this topic, what else would you want to know? What questions still linger for you? (2–3 questions—aim for big idea questions, not fact specific questions)

Required Readings

There are 3 required books for this course. They can be purchased through the bookstore or online. Additionally, books are also available at the library on reserve. Readings that are from the texts below are marked with an asterisks (*).

1) Mitra, D. (2017). *Educational Change and the Political Process*. New York: Routledge.

2) Manna, P., & McGuinn, P. (Eds.). (2013). *Education Governance for the Twenty-First Century: Overcoming the Structural Barriers to School Reform*. Brookings Institution Press.

3) McDermott, K. (2011). *High-Stakes Reform: The Politics of Educational Accountability*. Washington, D.C.: Georgetown Press.

All additional readings listed in the syllabus are available through the D2L website.

2) *Course Written Assignments*

WRITTEN ASSIGNMENT: EXAMINING THE POLICY MAKING PROCESS AND
GOVERNANCE CRITICAL REFLECTION AND ANALYSIS

These short (no more than 3 pages) assignments are meant to give you an early opportunity to synthesize and analyze material from this course. By providing feedback early on, I hope that you will be able to develop your reading, thinking and writing as the course progresses.

Please note the definition of critical being used in this assignment: critical— expressing or involving an analysis of the ***merits*** and ***faults*** of a work.

Keep in mind, a critical analysis is not meant to be negative. Being analytical is not the same as saying something is bad for all of these reasons. ALL research has limitations. Pointing out a limitation does not mean that the work is no longer extremely strong. Be careful not to become overly negative in your attempts at analyzing the works you read. Your ability to be analytical is derived from how you put together ideas, not simply how you poke holes in others' ideas.

An analysis paper asks the writer to make an argument about a particular book, article, or collection of research articles. The goal is two fold: one, identify and explain the argument that the author or authors are making, and two, provide your own argument about that argument or debate. One of the key directions of these assignments is to **avoid/minimize summary**—you are not writing a book report, but evaluating the readings.

Potential Questions to Consider in an Analysis of Readings

THEORETICAL QUESTIONS

- How does the author understand the situation? What is his/her theoretical background? How would this influence their view of the situation?
- Do the authors hold fundamentally different assumptions about the situation and how the world works?

DEFINITIONAL QUESTIONS

- Are all the concepts in the text clear? Does the author define a concept vaguely to allow it to travel across different situations? If a concept can relate two seemingly different situations, is the concept meaningful?
- Do the authors share the same definitions of key concepts? If not, is a comparison between the works "fair"?

EVIDENCE QUESTIONS

- Does the author's evidence support their argument? Do they have enough specific evidence to prove the more general point?
- Is there conflicting evidence to answer the question? If so, is one set of evidence more/less believable? Why? Are both sets of evidence potentially correct? Under what circumstances?
- Does the author underemphasize or ignore evidence that is contrary to their argument?
- Is the evidence credible? Can you identify a bias in the evidence?
- Was the study done by a political action committee, and environmental NGO, or a non-partisan research group? How might a group affiliation or funding influence the outcome of research?

IMPLICATION/POLICY RELEVANCE QUESTIONS

- What are the implications of this argument? Are those implications positive or negative? How has the author dealt with this issue?
- Are there other implications or limitations, which the author(s) did not address?

OTHER FACTORS TO CONSIDER

- Is the author's argument consistent throughout the book? Or, does the conclusion seem to offer a different argument than he/she presented in the introduction?
- Does the author's background have important implications for their argument?
- Do the specific language choices of the author betray a certain ideology or bias, or frame the argument in a certain way?
- Are the conclusions overstated or move beyond the evidence presented?
- How does the collection of research shed light on a larger topic or idea?
- What might be next steps in pursuing this line of research?

Structuring a Critical Reflection and Analysis Paper
Papers should begin with a short summary of the works and then dive into the argument. Since these papers are short, it is important to be concise in all parts of your analysis. Writing an outline (and following it) is crucial to remain focused on your argument and avoid summary or irrelevant description. Following is a sample outline for an analysis paper:

1) Introduction

   a. Identify the work(s) being analyzed
   b. Say something about the overarching theme(s) cutting across the articles or the main point you are focusing on.

    c. Present your argument and provide a preview of details—what are the steps you will take to prove your argument?

2) SHORT Summary of the Work(s)—Remember, I've read the piece— I don't need to read it again.

    a. Demonstrate you understand the piece and the argument/data provided by the author(s)

    b. Point out specific contributions/arguments for each article

    c. Present only what the reader needs to know to understand your argument

3) Your Argument

    a. Your argument will likely involve a number of sub-points you use to prove your larger argument.

    b. This should be the bulk of the paper—I want to read **your** argument about the work, not a summary.

4) Conclusion

    a. Reflect on your main point about the piece. Summarize and extend. This is where you can be bolder in your claims.

    b. Point out the importance of your argument (beyond it being a requirement for passing the class ☺)

Written Assignment: The Politics of Who Is/Should Be
in Charge of Schools

There are two parts to this assignment. However, the paper should be written as one coherent manuscript. Your introduction and thesis should set up both parts of the paper.

    Part 1: You are to describe and synthesize the course readings on the ever-present dilemma of who should control the US education system. What have you learned about who has influence, how and when? Identify the tensions that exist in the US system. Describe how these tensions have shifted and evolved over the past century. Explain any trade-offs between different goals of education when different groups have more/less power to control education in the US.

    Part 2, Option 1: Who should be in control of the US education system? Describe how you would set up the balance of power in the US education governance system. Identify how this balance of power aids the development of the education purposes (both educational and social) that you believe are important. Identify any weakness(es) or drawback(s) to your proposed governance system and argue why your model should be preferred despite this/these weakness(es).

Part 2, Option 2: Who has a better model? Compare and contrast the US governance system to that of another country. Explain the system with enough detail to support your argument for which system (either the US or a different country) is superior. What goals or purposes are both fostered and limited by the other country's system of governance. Argue why the one country's system is superior even though some goals may not be pursued.

Grades will be based on the following weighting scheme

Weekly Class Attendance: 10%
Weekly Class Participation: 20%
Critical Analysis: 30%
Governance Assignment: 40%

Please Note: A grade of "I" (incomplete) may be given only when the students (a) has completed at least 12 weeks of the semester but is unable to complete the class work and/or take the final examination because of illness or other compelling reasons; AND (b) had done satisfactory work in the course; AND (c) in the instructor's judgment can complete the required work without repeating the course. Grades of "I" will be given out rarely and students should speak with or email Professor Jacobsen as soon as possible if an issue arises.

Other Important Details

Students with disabilities: I will make reasonable accommodations for persons with documented disabilities. Please feel free to speak with me if there are issues of which I should be aware.

Academic Honesty and Integrity: We assume that students are honest and that all course work represents the student's own work. Violations of the academic integrity policy such as cheating, plagiarism, selling course assignments or academic fraud are grounds for academic action and/or disciplinary sanction as described in the University's student conduct code.

Incidents of Plagiarism: They will be taken very seriously and will be pursued. Students are strongly cautioned not to copy any text verbatim without appropriate quotations and source citations.

For University regulations on academic dishonesty and plagiarism, please refer to:

http://www.msu.edu/unit/ombud/plagiarism.html

MAKING FRIENDS, NOT JUST CONTACTS

In previous chapters, it has been noted that, all too often, school personnel such as teachers, principals, and other administrators are restricted from speaking out about school matters without the oversight of the school district's public relations director or school superintendent. In our opinion, this practice, unfortunately, speaks directly to what is viewed as a closed system. In most school systems, there is a large majority of personnel who are held accountable for working effectively with many other school personnel and often hundreds of students. This responsibility places them in the position of knowing a great deal about the schools' program successes and also its resource needs. In addition, such community contacts loom important.

Limiting the school's communication channels to one person or office inhibits the many valuable contacts that other competent school personnel experience. Yes, but might these persons say something that could open the door to some unwanted problem or cause confusion on the part of parents or community members? We submit that teachers and local school administrators are in the best position to speak on many school matters, are closer to the positive local schools' program accomplishments, and have the kind of professional judgments that project rather than inhibit community feedback.

GAINING POWER BY CREATING VIABLE
SCHOOL SYSTEM POLICIES AND
EFFECTIVE ADMINISTRATIVE REGULATIONS

It is clear that the control of school operations depends greatly on the body that controls policy adoption. When state legislatures, federal agencies, the courts, or other external agencies establish mandates or draft policies for school programs and operations via political actions, the power of the local school board is diminished. In addition, commitment is inhibited for externally developed policies. The extent to which the local school board assumes control over policy and administrative regulation development serves to define the extent to which it reserves its political power.

The terms *policy*, *regulation*, *bylaw*, and *rule* commonly are misused in educational communication and practices. It is quite frequent, for example, to hear a school principal speak of his or her school's education policies or for a school board to focus on its rules and administrative regulations. Failure of a school board to focus on its primary responsibility of the policy development process results in its intervention into administrative decision-making that belongs to the school superintendent and professional staff. It is clear, however, that a school board only has the authority delegated to it by the state, and, the school superintendent and professional staff have only the authority for developing administrative regulations that is given to them by the local school board.

DEFINING THE TERMS *SCHOOL POLICY* AND *ADMINISTRATIVE REGULATIONS*

Because of the paramount importance of policy and administration regulation development as related to local school control and power structure concerns, the following section centers on defining these terms and demonstrating methods of codifying them for governance purposes. We note at the outset that only the school board can adopt school policies, although it has become increasingly evident that state and federal government bodies, along with court decisions, have set forth local mandates for schools that find their way into school policies and administrative regulations.

The point here is just this: Without being deeply involved in school district policy development, governance power is absent in the school board's operations. "Policies are general in nature and call for a course of action to be taken by the school administration in meeting the desired purposes of the educational program" (Norton, 2017, p. 5). A policy can be identified by determining the extent to which it contains the following ten characteristics:

A policy is

1. an assertion of a goal(s), purpose(s), or an aim(s);
2. related to a general area of prime importance;
3. equivalent to legislation;
4. applicable over long periods of time;
5. a broad statement that allows for freedom of interpretation and execution;
6. mainly the concern of the school board;
7. a strategy undertaken to solve or ameliorate a problem or need;
8. concerned with topics of vital interest to the citizenry;
9. related to the question of *what* to do;
10. gives guidance for the school superintendent but leaves room for his or her discretionary action.

An administrative regulation is

1. related to a specific problem area of administration; it is a procedure to carry out a policy;

2. mainly the concern of the professional staff;
3. a precise statement calling for exact interpretation and execution;
4. related to the question of *how* to do;
5. executive in nature but ultimately under the legislative authority of the school board.

A rule is

1. a standard statement, other than a policy or regulation, that is set forth by an administrative unit within the school district or local school for the primary purpose of implementing an administrative regulation; specifies a required action as to what is to be done, when it is to be done, and commonly who is to do it;
2. a statement of behavior and/or activity that specifies personnel or student actions but does not conflict with either school policies or administrative regulations;
3. related to the question of how a regulation such as student control is to be enforced in a school environment.

A by-law is

1. a combination of laws and parliamentary procedure;
2. like any other rule, which specifies required action that leaves little room for individual judgments;
3. a rule that relates to internal operations of the board of education. A by-law might read that "the school board shall meet on each first and third Wednesdays of each month to consider the business matters that require board action, hearing first and second readings of proposed policies, and adopting policies that require board approval."
4. related to the question of how the board will govern itself (Norton, 2017, pp. 4–5).

THE CODIFICATION OF POLICIES AND ADMINISTRATIVE REGULATIONS: A POWER FACTOR

It is beyond the scope of this chapter to set forth a detailed discussion relating to how school policies and administrative regulations are classified. But, give a moments' thought to the problem of placing books on a library's shelves without some way to code them by a rational relationship and easy location. The well-known Dewey Decimal Classification system was first implemented for libraries more than 142 years ago and revised and extended many times over the years. Yet, new classification methods are constantly being implemented in libraries to facilitate the handling of new books and electronic reading materials.

Two policy codification systems were set forth for classifying school policies and regulations, one, a first edition, by Davies and Brickell in 1957 and another by the National School Boards Association that has been revised several times since its first publication as early as 1970. These systems have served historically as the foundation for classifying school policies and regulation.

The Nation School Boards Association Alpha system (1991) uses letters rather than numbers to code policy and regulation entries. The NEPN/NSBA policy sections are:

A   Foundations and Basic Commitments
B   School Board Operations
C   General School Administration
D   Fiscal Management
E   Business Management/Support Services
F   Fiscal Development
G   Personnel
H   Negotiations/Meet and Confer
I   Instructional Program
J   Students
K   School Community Relations
L   Educational Agencies Relations
M   Relations with Other Organizational Agencies

Codification systems have six major parts, section, subsection, division, subdivision, item, and sub-item. For example, the code GCAAC refers to the section personnel, the third subsection "C," first division "A," first subdivision "A," and third item "C." In a policy manual, the series of Personnel has the subsection Personal Staff, division Professional Staff Positions, subdivision Instructional Staff Positions, and third item Resource Staff Positions. Of course, one would have to have the entire Personnel section to be able to see the comprehensive topical listings in that section. A major advantage of the alpha system is that it has 26 letters for classification entries. The following Davies-Brickell system is Arabic and used only nine numbers for coding. Using more than nine numbers poses problems that will be noted in the following section.

The nine sections of the Davies-Brickell Codification system are:

• 1000 Community Relations
• 2000 Administration
• 3000 Business and Non-Instructional Operations
• 4000 Personnel
• 5000 Students

- 6000 Instruction
- 7000 New Construction
- 8000 internal Board Policies
- 9000 Bylaws

Similar to the NASB system, the first letter is the section, second letter is the subsection, third letter is the division, fourth letter is the subdivision, and the fifth letter is the first item. Assume that you wanted to classify a policy dealing with elementary grades, curriculum, and curriculum guides. The 6000 series of the Davis & Brickell code system is Instruction. The first subsection under instruction is #1, Elementary and Secondary. The fourth division under Elementary and Secondary is #4, Curriculum, and the third entry under Curriculum is #3, Curriculum Guides, which results in code 6143.

If more than nine entries were needed under any subsection, division, subdivision, or item in the Davies-Brickell system, the number 10 or above could not be used. Assume that one code was 614 and it needed 10 subdivisions. If the number 61410 was entered, at best it would appear to indicate 1 subdivision and zero items. Or, if a decimal were used, it would incorrectly be coded as 6141.0. Thus, the Davies-Brickell classification system is confined to the use of only nine numbers. In the alpha system, however, J, K, L, M, N, O, etc. represent numbers 10, 11, 12, 13, 14, 15 and go up to letter Z or 26 entries.

Confused? A little practice will overcome it. Write the code for an entry in the Davies-Brickell system for section 6 personnel, third subsection, first division, fourth subdivision and second item. It's personnel, "6," 6314.2. Take time to find and open a copy of your school district's policy manual. What codification system does it use? Read one section of the policy manual. Does it make more sense to you now? Could you explain its organization to others? Of course, one would have to have a complete series of the classification being used to identify its contents.

What is the primary and most important benefit that is gained by a school board relating to policy development? The answer is more control and increased power and authority. What do the school superintendent and professional staff gain from developing and implementing the school district's administrative regulations? The answer is more freedom to exercise his or her own discretion in the decision-making process and using the professional knowledge and skills required for meeting the day-to-day issues and problems that occur in the operation of effective school systems.

However, might the *division of labor* between the policy responsibilities of the school board and the administrative responsibilities of the school superintendent lead to a problem between the board and the superintendent? On the contrary, this division of labor leads to an understanding of the work of the school board and the related work of the school superintendent. Empirical evidence has shown that such division lines that exist between the board and superintendent fosters positive relations. When each party focuses on doing its job well, everyone, including the school departments, faculty, staff, and students, benefits.

OTHER COMMUNITY INVOLVEMENTS

It is common for a school superintendent to be a member of a civic club in the school community, and the assistant superintendent might be a member of one of the several clubs or groups that exist. Many of the important business CEOs, industrial managers, and city government officials commonly are members of such groups. Members of these clubs have children in the local schools, and the club is often asked to support one of the schools' many program activities. Important school information can be disseminated in these settings as well as the ability to learn the opinions of various educational issues that confront the school district.

We would submit that more teachers and school principals should be supported in joining civic clubs and other groups whereby important relationships can be developed, and active support on such matters as bond issues and needed facility improvements can be clarified as well. Who benefits? Both parties benefit; the school personnel and the club members. One example might serve to explain how such attendance can help to clarify matters and set the record straight on misunderstandings that often are disseminated in group sessions.

A school superintendent of a school district in the state of Kansas was a member of the city's Rotary Club. The guest speaker spoke on the topic of the poor business programs in the nation's public schools and told of the research on students' lack of knowledge of business matters. In fact, as stated by the guest speaker, in one test of senior high school students, the students thought that the percentage of profit on business sales was from 50 percent to 200 percent, a gross exaggeration. Of course, the majority of Rotary members was business people. It is difficult to state their surprise and frustration relative to this stated finding.

At the end of the Rotary meeting, the editor of the local newspaper approached the school superintendent and indicated that he had better do something about this poor understanding of business in their schools. Rotary club members were not going to "let go" of this information, and the schools were going to face a great deal of criticism. The school superintendent indeed initiated a follow-up of the information set forth by the guest speaker. The speaker's research, reportedly, was done by a university in Florida. The superintendent contacted officials at the Florida State Department and two universities in the state. None of these sources had ever heard of the university that reportedly had done the research or the university in question.

The school superintendent contacted the editor of the local newspaper and told him of his follow-up information reports. He wisely suggested that the editor follow-up on this matter himself. The editor spent considerable time in doing so. At the next meeting of the Rotary Club, the editor asked for the floor. He reported that there was no evidence that the reported research actually took place. This editor's report ended any concern that was on the minds of the club members. To our knowledge, no additional follow-up regarding the speaker or the "fake study" was heard of again. We do present the story as being true and factual.

POLITICS: A VITAL FORCE IN EDUCATION

It is clear that the force of politics has been noticed in education historically. An early article by Karns (1970) is a case in point. Karns opens his comments by stating, "No segment of American government is so thoroughly political as the schools. The effects of political activity are felt in every American school system regardless of its size or composition. Teachers and educators must realize they are not outside the body politic in a protected tower; they are in the center of the political arena" (p. 38).

Karns believes that a successful superintendent must be more than an educator. He or she must be a shrewd politician. He too believes that educators have been naïve regarding power structures in their communities. It looms important that educators become acquainted with their legislators. We refer back to the discussion of course work in educational administration that focused on following the state legislative session activity relative to education.

Not only would such a course provide beneficial benefits relative to analyzing the politics of education but would develop important insights into the educational views of the legislators representing the community and state. Being well informed of who is representing the educational bills, the content of the education bills, and who wins and who loses the passage of the education bills serves to open the door for intelligent communication by the school leaders.

State administrator and teacher associations must upgrade their involvement in the political arena as well. Such involvement necessitates much more than just keeping abreast of legislative educational activities. For example, one state director of the administrators' association installed a "radio system" in his office that followed the actions of the state legislature relative what it was doing on educational matters. What he really needed to do was to be involved in what was going to be introduced educationally as opposed to just learning what the legislature had decided after the fact. Another state director of an administrators' association stated that she was not able to deal with state education political matters. If she did so, the association would lose its tax-exempt status. Something is wrong here.

HOW TO IMPROVE THE POLITICAL SKILLS WITHIN THE WORKFORCE

An informative article by V. Marie Vicher (2007) focused on the importance of improving the political savvy of personnel in the workplace. It appears to be of vital importance that the political savvy of school system workers be in place before attempts to identify external power influentials can be successful. Vicher asks the question as to whether or not political skills are teachable or are innate. She contends that political savvy can indeed be taught in the classroom. She does note, however, that political savvy in the workplace has been called by different names: political intelligence, political astuteness, political ability, and political acumen. Thus, some authorities compare political savvy to effective leadership that reveals practical intelligence or perhaps just common sense.

The literature suggests that political savvy development in education appears to be mostly left to chance with little or no education or training. It is not systematically taught in the workplace because organizational politics seemed not to be openly practiced (Truty, 2006). Nevertheless, authorities have expressed the opinion that political savvy should be instituted in order to provide a safe place for free and deliberate unveiling, exploration, discussion, strategizing, and criticizing of office politics. Such skill is a necessary element for leadership success even though there is a lack of coaching offered to develop such skill.

There is a common belief that political skill is learned by trial and error or it depends on self-development. Nevertheless, the general belief on the part of researchers is that it indeed can be developed. Some authorities contend that the teaching of political skill should not be left to chance but should be addressed systematically within the educational system. Classes should be developed and offered to students at the high school level and the undergraduate students at the college level with emphasis on what it is and how to develop it. We agree with this contention.

The individual school leader can enhance his or her political savvy or intelligence by implementing three behaviors that increase one's political influence. The following five strategies closely parallel the characteristics of effective change administration: (1) Establishing an appealing *vision statement* that sets forth what the school or school system wants to become. It is future oriented and establishes a guiding statement for developing a *mission statement* that sets forth the steps that must be taken to achieve the school's vision. (2) What program activities will be pursued? (3) What specific program areas will be emphasized? (4) What standards must be realized? and (5) What changes in the present program must be addressed?

Answers to each of the foregoing strategies conjure up problems and issues that require astute political knowledge and skill. A new set of values must be articulated. The leader must demonstrate the characteristics of self-sacrifice, new behaviors, and illustrations of courage and conviction about the vision that is guided by effective political knowledge and skill. Such skill is demonstrated by the leader's astuteness and social intelligence. As stated by Truty (2006), "Political skill is defined as astuteness and social intelligence in the workplace; political savvy assumes the existence of the inevitability of office politics" (p. 13). And, as Truty argues, formal skill development for political savvy ought to be offered students and workers at all organizational levels to include formal education curriculum.

DECISIONS, DECISIONS, DECISIONS:
AN EFFECTIVE POLITICAL LEADER
MAKES AND KEEPS THEM IN PRACTICE

Having control of the decision-making process is a common practice for gaining power within the organization. Such control is exemplified in having control of what topics are placed or are not placed on the meeting agendas. In some cases, consideration of one agenda item might be strategically placed on the agenda so as the group's discussion is centered on other issues. Controlling the appointment of members to subcommittees that are of the same opinion as the leader serves a controlling purpose as well.

Decision-making models have been set forth in the literature for many years: (1) clarify the problem; (2) gather the facts; (3) determine the options; and on, and on. Most every decision carries some political considerations with it. The need for the school leader is to assume the responsibility and take the actions that will serve to retain the decision in practice. We recommend the following procedures for helping each leader not only make a viable decision but to meet the greater challenge of implementing and keeping it in practice.

Many decisions are intuitive in nature. One's knowledge and experience automatically give the person an answer for what to do. Others are more complex and political in nature and call for improvement changes in worker behaviors and how things are done. An attempt to implement such changes quickly is met commonly by misunderstanding, confusion, and defiance.

Such decisions require time to give one's best thought to the matter at hand. What might happen if I don't make a decision immediately? Might I be able to use better judgment and make a best decision?

What additional information and/or data are needed in this case? What is the best source for gathering the needed information? Who will be affected by the decision, and how might these persons be involved? What parties need to be informed of the issue at hand and told of how the issue will affect them? Why is this matter important for the accomplishment of our mission? What professional development will be needed on the part of school personnel? What kinds of interventions, changes, and resources will be needed to have a successful implementation of the decision? How will the school program, students, and school personnel benefit by this change?

Openness regarding change within the organization facilitates trust and cooperation among employees. Empirical research has made it clear that high performers in the organization favor opportunities to grow and develop. In fact, if self-improvement activities are not available in the organization, such talent will look for such opportunities elsewhere. Depending on the matter/ issue at hand, members within the organization might be able to take the lead in accomplishing the changes in question. Retaining the talent in the school system is a leading political priority in the contemporary competitive business world.

The question as to whether a group of individuals can increase the quality of decisions made by individuals looms important. The answer to this question was set forth in a doctoral dissertation by William Bombeck (1974) over four decades ago. Organizational development concepts of virtual teams, system's thinking, and transactional analysis tend to be supported by Bombeck's research results. Using over 80 participants, a large variety of strategies and decision-making exercises, only 7 of the individuals had better individual scores than the average of the team's scores. A comparison of team and individual scores supported the superiority of team efforts.

POLITICS AND THE FUTURE OF EDUCATION

Several issues that will face education in the next decade will be noted in this concluding chapter. Although we do not have a crystal ball to forecast the outcome of the issues, it is clear that the hand of politics will determine the outcome of each one. We begin by considering public school curriculum and how it is to be pursued. Have you ever given thought to making lifelong education compulsory? Finland is one of the countries that have done so. What about requiring local school districts to be largely supported by local and private funds including family education payments? Or, what about viewing education taking place under the guidance of educators, but learners may educate themselves?

What about viewing education as any experience that has a formative effect on the way the student thinks and can take place in many places other than a classroom? Currently, students are educated in formal settings such as classrooms with a teacher in charge of what is to be learned. Other forms of education are emerging, although alternative systems have existed for hundreds of years.

We make special note of the emerging or re-emerging views of education that carry with them political implications that are certain to be faced by school leaders. There is considerable talk about changes that are needed in current formal education. *Formal education* takes place in a structured program of school grades, classrooms with students at desks, and a certified teacher in front. Informal education might take place in a variety of different places such as a museum or other place outside of a classroom. The learner might be guided by an experienced individual or be involved in a self-learning activity. The term *autodidacticism* describes self-directed learning. The person doing self-learning is termed an *autodidact*. Well-known individuals such as Abraham Lincoln, Charles Darwin, Thomas Alva Edison, George Bernard Shaw, Michael Faraday, and Leonardo da Vinci are viewed as self-learners.

The factor of ongoing, rapid social and economic change has necessitated the need to assume other less time-consuming ways for student learning often termed *phenomenon-based learning*. This kind of learning might take place in a stock market exchange office or through specific studies of subjects such as hospital management, environment management, aging, diversity, and poverty.

Attacks on the present public school education outcomes have prompted many groups to recommend and establish other ways to educate children and youth. Thoughts have arisen regarding the need to make education a lifelong requirement. Many alternatives to the formal education system, including extended home schooling, alternative schools, Montessori schools, charter schools, cooking schools, business schools, vocational schools, agricultural schools, preparation schools, and others, are among the long list of education alternatives. For each of the alternative education programs, there are opponents who point to their deficiencies and berate them for encouraging students to leave common public schools.

PUBLIC EDUCATION FUNDING
BY THE LOCAL, STATE, AND FEDERAL GOVERNMENTS
VS. PRIVATE SCHOOLS AND FAMILIES

The question of who is to fund education will continue to be a significant political debate in the years ahead. Funding inequalities will be near the top of financial support politics relative to education of children and youth. Whether financial support is in relation to per-pupil funding, vouchers, school choice, equalization, private or public education, student achievement, ability to pay measures, vocational education, accountability, cost effectiveness, or other arrangements and provisions, politics will be at the forefront of financial support decisions. The literature commonly focuses on the importance of understanding the political climate of the market for LCPS (low-cost private schools). For example, how can relationships of power and accountability between users, government, and private providers produce better education outcomes for low-income citizens?

SCHOOL CHOICE AND POLITICS: PUBLIC SCHOOLS? VOUCHERS? PRIVATE SCHOOLS? CHARTER SCHOOLS? VOCATIONAL SCHOOLS?

The "war" is on concerning school choice and how K–12 schools are to be operated in states throughout the nation. In one state, for example, since 2012, public school enrollment has increased by less than 1 percent. On the other hand, public charter schools, which operate independently of districts and their rules, have increased nearly 50 percent. In fact, in Arizona, charter schools now have four times as many students as private schools. Private school enrollment has not increased substantially. Of course, in some states the ability to open charter schools is far more limited. And, in addition, more reports of failing charter schools are being noted in several states. In Arizona, for example, charter schools have closed suddenly in the middle of the school year leaving students to scramble for entry in public school programs.

Ways for learning continue to be proposed and debated. *Formal learning*, commonly carried out in classrooms with a teacher in front; *alternative education,* which is a broad concept that includes methods from self-learning to alternative schools of various kinds; *indigenous education,* which focuses on regaining the cultures, languages, and values of a community; *informal learning,* which takes place in a variety of settings whereby active learning can take place; *self-directed learning,* which is realized by activities of the "learner" and accomplished by him or her; and *open education,* which is carried out by modern electronic educational technology are learning strategies that have been implemented historically for student learning. Which methods are to be implemented depends largely on the culture of the school community and the politics within it.

A study by the DaVinci Institute makes claims that it has the answer. As stated by the DaVinci Institute (2007, March 3), "The pace of change is mandating that we produce a faster, smarter, better grade of human beings. Current systems are preventing that from happening. Future education system will be unleashed with the advent of a standardized rapid courseware-builder and a single point global distribution system" (p. 1). In brief, the institute argues that present systems are preventing us from doing great things. The missing pieces, according to the institute, are the standard architect for an organic coursework module and the software necessary to build the coursework. In the end, the general public will be able to build coursework on any imaginable topic.

In summary, the emphasis will be placed on learning rather than teaching. Coursework will be created by experts, and the student will determine the most comfortable time and place, including the pace, of the learning. Teachers might be available to serve as guides or coaches as opposed to subject experts. As coaches, the coach commonly serves to ask the question, "Where do you want to go?" By being a good listener, the coach asks key questions, coaches students, and encourages action toward the learner's goals. Such broad questions and their answers commonly lead toward certain specifics that serve the student to develop priorities, and to identify his or her personal strengths and life opportunities.

WHERE SHOULD IT ALL BEGIN?

Historically, reading, mathematics, science, foreign language, vocational education, and physical education have been foremost among the curricular topics identified by our nation's presidents and others as being essential in the nation's K–12 curricular programs. But what about the current need for student understanding for democracy and citizenship? We submit that contemporary incidents of volatile student behaviors, racial issues, and other citizenship are evidence of the need for much more emphasis on civics in the local school programs nationally. Alicia Brown (2011, April 14) perhaps has said it best: "A curriculum view could see the end to citizenship as a required subject. It is not to assume that young people will somehow acquire this knowledge" (p. 1).

She comments further that citizenship as a subject can serve to motivate and inform young people into becoming more thoughtful concerning their role in positive citizenship and their importance in participating in public life. In order to acquire such knowledge, young persons must be educated in it. We recommend that public schools nationally require the subject of civics in all grades K–12. A great deal of the learning should take place in the practices of democracy within the practices of school programming. All children and youth must come to the thought of what it means to be a citizen of the United States.

EDUCATION BY DESIGN:
INNOVATION WITH A PURPOSE:
WHAT DOES REIMAGINING HAVE TO DO WITH IT?

If you haven't read or heard about *reimagining*, you haven't been reading or listening. Today, in education, the password for innovation is reimagining. Recent publications have included books on reimagining education, reimagining language arts, reimagining the future of education, reimagining library spaces, reimagining writing assessment, reimagining science, reimagining mathematics classrooms, reimagining business education, reimagining schools, reimagining teaching, reimagining faith education, and reimagining most everything else. The topic of reimagining is discussed here since its contentions hold many implications for power politics and the purposes of this chapter.

REIMAGINING AND DESIGNING
THE FUTURE EDUCATION WORKFORCE:
A FOCUS ON ROLE PREPARATION

The primary question to be addressed is whether or not we have organized all education roles from small-group reading teachers to playground supervisors. In a new model of preparation, anyone working with students would need to demonstrate proficiency in the knowledge, skills, and dispositions associated with the role they are filling. For some roles, this preparation may be relatively short and in other cases, much more robust. In all cases it should be grounded in specific competencies and that these competencies should be seen as part of a larger set, such that educators could "stack" competencies to access opportunities for larger or sophisticated roles that would be associated with greater responsibility and compensation.

For those who choose to be lifelong educators, thought must be given to new ways for them to continually develop in personalized ways and signal their expertise. Like doctors and lawyers, educators would be expected to develop specialties. Educators would be seen as experts in their various specialties and viewed as an important part of effective team-based staffing models. In sum, a preparation system for new educator roles must be competency-based, personalized, and interoperable—allowing educators to flexibly move between roles as a function of what they believe, know, and are able to do.

Presently, there are approximately 3,860,270 K–12 teachers in public, charter, and private schools. Reimagining the workforce proposals for that many teachers certainly would hold major concerns for this political force.

No one possesses a "magic wand" to get such reimagining accomplished. Questions such as the following must be addressed and answered: (1) What does 21st century look like? (2) What kinds of roles and talent are required to deliver it? (3) How do we invite a diverse group of adults into these new roles while simultaneously elevating the profession? (4) How do we prepare creative respective professionals who can work in teams and deliver better learning outcomes and experiences to the communities?

Our specific questions would be, would current non-educators, but prospective teachers, really know and understand what teachers really do? And, even though role changes are proposed in the reimagining of the workforce, is expertise as a reading teacher or other teacher specialists prepared to handle student discipline, student bullying, substance abuse problems, parental complaints, controlled curriculum mandates from the state and federal agencies, and the ability to withstand an eight-hour day and five days a week of teaching or service inside or outside a school classroom? Great teachers possess both affective and cognitive characteristics.

A book by Norton (2015) listed thirty-seven affective and twenty cognitive characteristics of great teachers. The leading affective skills included caring/ loving, positive classroom climate, communication skills, enthusiasm, motivation of students, sense of humor, good listening skills, teaching experience, and high verbal ability. The unlicensed teacher might possess all but one of these important *affective* skills. The highest *cognitive* skills of great teachers were reported as high subject knowledge, high expectations for standards and goals, command of the field, enthusiasm, student achievement goals, organization skills, effective teaching strategies, monitoring of student learning, student motivation, and the meeting of student needs. This information is clear to point out that subject knowledge alone is not enough to guarantee teaching success.

REIMAGINING AND CHANGE:
SIMILAR BUT PERHAPS DIFFERENT

Reimagining is to imagine again or renew so as to form a new conception of the concept or practice. *Change,* on the other hand, is to make or become different. A concept or practice is altered so as to make it different. Changes within our school commonly are discussed from three perspectives: (1) mandated changes set forth by state and federal agencies and court ruling; (2) changes that commonly take place from everyday internal and external factors that are encountered continuously in the school community; and (3) program/practice changes that are outcomes of the school's implementation of planned program's assessments that call for program improvements. Reimagining, on the other hand, commonly calls for a complete new procedure for doing things that call for a new improved way of organizing and/or carrying out of a program or organizational process.

Commonly, change is put into action when program improvement is the guiding purpose. Reimagining is implemented when the current program is not working and/or the vision of the school is not being met under the present program concepts and practices. A total renewal of organizational concepts is in order. New personnel roles must be defined. New innovative personnel roles and team strategies and new team-building arrangements must be put into operation that overcome the current deficiencies and fail to fulfill organizational purposes.

New provisions and personnel roles must be put into place in order to attract and retain talented personnel. System thinking, whereby a conceptual framework, a body of knowledge, and strategies are established, will serve to make patterns of program purposes is made clear to all concerned. Competency-based performance relates to the abilities and/or factors that make an individual qualified to perform a specialized task with confidence and at a required level of performance.

TEAM-BASED CROSS-DISCIPLINARY RESEARCH

We give high hopes for the advancement of educational research in the reimagination of school programs nationally. If, indeed, new roles, programs, and procedures are to be implemented, not only is the procedure of planning of primary importance, but ongoing assessment strategies and team-based research must accompany it. The actions of "let's just do it and think about researching it later" will end in negative results. Pilot programs accompanied by an effective research component should precede any reimagination of a major educational intervention.

Neither the university colleges of education nor the local schools are presently prepared to carry out research necessary for this "mandate." Very few, if any, higher education programs are presently prepared to assume this research objective. Such a goal cannot be fulfilled by the end of the year survey, or other over simplification of program results will suffice. A program of ongoing action research under the supervisions of highly qualified personnel is essential. Where is this caliber of research personnel to be found? How are they to be supported? How prepared are local school district now to implement effective research at the local school level? Most every school district that joins a reimagining education program has a long way to go to just be at the starting gate. Such a start, however, is long overdue. Unless major changes are realized in research efforts by universities and local schools, program innovations are likely to once again fade away.

THE TWO PRIMARY POSITIONS CONCERNING THE PURPOSES OF EDUCATION

We close the discussion of reimagining education by underscoring two primary positions most commonly set forth for establishing the purposes of education in the United States. The history of legislative involvement in education and the nature of the political support for education are framed around the political support afforded these two positions.

Position 1 has stressed the value of education to the individual emphasizing its potential for positively influencing students' personal development, promoting autonomy, forming cultural identity, and establishing a career or occupation.

Position 2 has emphasized education's contributions to societal purposes, including good citizenship, shaping students into productive members of society, promoting society's general economic development, and preserving cultural values (Winch & Gingell, 2008). Position 1 places emphasizes on the individual and his or her opportunities through education. Position 2 emphasizes the importance of the educated citizen for fostering the concept of democracy and free enterprise in the United States. Although both purposes are of paramount importance, educational programs to deliver the purposes tend to differ and their support financially enters the crowded arena that is determined politically.

A WORD ABOUT ACTION RESEARCH: CHECK PLEASE

Action research appears to fit well with reimagining in relation to its view of collaborative procedures carried out by those professionals with a shared educational concern. Such a collaborative research effort serves to develop a systematic, inquiring approach toward a team's own practices and to make a positive change in what the team has been doing. Preparation for ongoing action research must be provided in the requirements of degree programs in teacher and administrator preparation programs. The implementation of reimagining concepts will succeed only if it is accompanied by effective and ongoing research results.

Assume that the action research team wanted to investigate the matter of learning styles that existed within the student group. Several planning and implement steps must be considered: (1) What specific focus concerning learning styles do we want to examine? (2) What are the different learning styles that research has found among students of our age group? (3) What specific questions do we want to address in our investigation? (4) What procedures will be most effective in finding the information that we seek? What specific observations, presentations, and learning behavior data do we have to gather? How will the data be treated, and who will be able to "read" the results? How will validity and reliability be determined? (6) How do we plan to disseminate the action research findings? (7) How will the findings be addressed in the implementation of our instructional programming?

In any case, the first question of paramount importance to be addressed is, are the university or school district personnel aware of the sophisticated student learning styles research by Pashler et al. (2008)? If not, this major study will shed light on the topic at hand. An additional question regarding student learning styles to be considered is the following: Is the university or school district really prepared to implement the research expertise necessary to investigate student learning styles?

As concluded by the major study of Pashler and associates, "The contrast between the enormous popularity of learning-styles within education and the lack of credible evidence for its utility is, in our opinion, striking and disturbing. If classification of students' learning styles has practical utility, it remains to be demonstrated" (p. 119). The researchers stated that they had been unable to find any evidence that meets the standard research procedures recommended in their study.

This chapter has considered many changes that are viewed in relation to the future of education. The presence of politics is woven into most every effort to meet the forthcoming issues and their related problems. The individual with little political knowledge and skill most likely will not survive as an educational leader. In addition, many countries are now drastically changing the way their citizens are being educated (Wikipedia, 2018). Some knowledge becomes outdated, and new knowledge is being addressed as quickly and easily as possible. Such developments as phenomenon-based learning are being introduced whereby such concepts as outer space travel and climate change are studied and compulsory Pre–K–16–CLL learning is enforced (pre-kindergarten to compulsory lifelong learning).

WHAT IS MICRO-CREDENTIALING AND HOW CAN IT WORK WITH MY 25 TEACHERS?

A new book or two are needed in an effort to begin to understand the focus of reimagining when it comes to understanding terms such as *micro-credentialing, creation stage, technological platforms, online modules, ideation stage,* and other related terms important in the process of reimagining education. The term *micro-credentialing* has been described as an effort to make professional development more personalized, engaging, and relevant to teachers. Claims include the contention that it is a lot more focused and practical than stereo-typed education classes. One has to show how the learning applies right now according to the cheerleaders for this new credentialing effort.

We address this topic because of its potential for becoming a major political issue nationally.

We asked one "specialist" just how a school principal with one assistant principal and four department chairs could initiate micro-credentialing in his or her school. The specialist responded by saying, "The micro-credentials would be focused on online modules. These are in the early ideation stage at this time, but it has a lot of potential. Online still provides opportunity for mentorship, group work, and individual study, but will be augmented and tracked by technological platforms." In other words, we don't know.

Presently, most institutions of higher education "prepare" and then recommend teachers for licensure. The State Department of Education or other official state agencies, in turn, approve the teacher's license. Just how the licensing process would work with micro-credentialing is not clear to us at this time. Three questions appear to be important: (1) Who or what bodies actually are given the authority to prepare prospective teachers in the micro-credentialing process? Is this authority given to the local school system? Higher education institutions? The State Education Department? Some other credentialing body? (2) If person A is micro-credentialed in the state of Arizona, how might this licensure process be accepted in any other state, perhaps a state that has not endorsed this licensing process? and (3) What research studies have set forth the basis for the implementation of the foregoing concepts?

A CLOSING NOTE OF CAUTION

In our extensive research efforts relative to the contents of this book, we came across a comprehensive article by John Hattie titled *What Doesn't Work in Education: The Politics of Distraction* (2015). We recommend the reading of this work to educators specifically and to others interested in educational improvements generally. Few articles give rise to more serious thoughts on improving education in schools than this one. Hattie's article makes one think about one's own professional convictions on educational matters and all of the contentions set forth relative to what we are doing in our attempts to improve education for children and youth. It raises the question "Will education ever get serious about its need to place research in a priority position in its decision making process?"

Hattie (2015) gives us caution when it comes to structural fixes (e.g., more money, open vs. traditional instructional classrooms, different types of buildings, setting standards, more assessments, more technology, lower class size, greater school choice, longer school days, performance pay, additional summer school, matching style of learning to individual students, individualized instruction, ability grouping, charter schools, student retention and other so-called fixes for improving education). Hattie discusses research findings for these and other innovations that he terms wasted good intentions. Do we really know the likely outcomes of the intervention being proposed, or is it based only on our high hopes?

As underscored by Hattie (2015), "The argument is not that any of these solutions are irrelevant, wrong, or mischievous, but that an overemphasis on one or all of them creates a distraction from other, more critical, or effective ways for educational systems to become world-class" (p. 7). Hattie notes that such "innovations" have minimal effect on improving student learning. What these "innovations" tend to do is to distract school leaders and university instructors from implementing policies or teaching principles that can actually make a significance difference. In this chapter, we have noted the importance of local school policy making and other educational practices that do lead to learning improvement.

KEY CHAPTER IDEAS AND RECOMMENDATIONS

- Schools and school systems are political systems and vary according to the political principles employed.
- By attempting to understand the detailed politics of organizational life we are able to grasp important qualities of organizations that are often glossed over.
- The turning over of policy development to external parties must stop.
- Non-involvement is not the right answer for education leaders. If practiced, school leaders will find themselves outside the circle of positive change.
- Open systems of communication are of paramount importance for schools and school systems. A closed communication position shuts the door to many valuable contacts.
- The importance of local policy development cannot be overly emphasized. Local control depends on a school board's ability to develop and implement school policies that serve the purposes of the school community.
- In-service education programs are highly recommended for school board members for learning the importance of policy development and preserving some semblance of local control.

- When effective policy and administrative regulation development is in place at the local school level, the school board benefits by having more control and the school superintendent gains more freedom to act.
- State and local teacher associations must increase their involvement in the political world.
- Having control of the decision-making process at the local school level is a common practice for school boards and the professional staff to gain control.
- Political savvy can be improved.
- Reimagining school roles of working professionals is a contemporary strategy in education. Lifelong learning is a growing concern.
- Educational improvement emphasizes learning rather than teaching. Educational improvement should be emphasizing effective research and not resting on its reputation of innovative practices.
- College and universities are not standing still in regard to educational renewal. Reimagining education is the growing development of the 21st century. Related research continues to lag behind.
- New workforce roles are being introduced for teachers, and team instruction strategies are being utilized in innovative efforts to improve student learning. In some instances, however, the introduction of personnel into education programs who are not licensed through high standard procedures must be avoided. Placing personnel in schools to learn about teaching and administration rather than being prepared for such roles in effective higher education programs is problematic. Major criticisms of education nationally center on what is termed our ineffective schools. An aspiring teacher or administrator being instructed in such situations just results in having the learner learn more of the same.
- Instructional strategies are focusing on teachers' expertise, competency-based, personalized, and inter-operational methods that allow for flexibility for moving between instructional roles.
- Reimagining is to imagine again or renew so as to form an innovative concept or practice.
- Reimagining is implemented when the current program is not working. However, reimagining without controlled pilot programs that are effectively researched is problematic at best.
- Ongoing research, including action research, looms important for evaluating and assessing reimagining program results. Qualified research personnel and research units should be operated within each local school district in the United States or available to the school district as an outsource facility. Program innovation without prior and ongoing research is an exercise in futility.
- It is highly recommended that all public schools in grades K–12 give additional instruction on civic education. The knowledge and skills required for

becoming an effective citizen, understanding the importance of the American democracy, knowing how a democratic government works, and developing the knowledge and skills required for being effective in the political world must be a continuous educational goal from the early grades through high school graduation and beyond.

DISCUSSION QUESTIONS

1. Give thought to the time your school, or one with which you are most familiar, was considering or confronted by a matter regarding a school rule, a program offering, or a new school activity such as recess or student discipline. Who was supporting or "pressing" the issue, and how was it ultimately decided? What was the nature of the ultimate politics surrounding the matter? What group or individual was most influential in making the final decision?

2. Describe the extent to which you and your school leaders are prepared to deal with political matters that are encountered in curriculum decisions, student behavior, grading procedures, student achievement, and other program activities. Rate the political savvy that you believe was present or practiced by school leaders in the issue(s).

3. Consider your personal involvement in the decision-making process as a professional member of the school district. For example, how involved have you been in the decision-making process relative to policies and procedures? Briefly describe this involvement.

4. To what extent have you had the opportunity to speak externally about the status of school accomplishments, needs, innovations, or other matters? Please describe the extent to which you and other faculty personnel are permitted to speak to external groups on school issues being faced.

5. Information in this chapter has contended that the emphasis should be placed on student learning rather than teaching. How do you interpret this contention, and what does it mean to you?

6. Assume that someone asks you about a new term reimagining in education. How would you respond? Take a moment to write out what major points that you would make in explaining the term to others.

7. The topic of research was supported in this chapter as being of primary importance. Rate your school or school district on its research activities on a scale of 1 low to 5 high. Then support your selection by using specific evidence.

8. Quickly review the chapter's inclusion of Rebecca Jacobsen's university course on the politics of education. Write a paragraph or two on your analysis of the courses purposes and contents. For example, what information would be most beneficial for you personally?

9. Other countries have given thought to making lifelong education compulsory. What is your reaction to such a proposal for the United States?
10. This chapter stated a primary goal as focusing on ways school leaders can increase their political knowledge and skills. What specific content in the chapter was most effective in meeting this goal for you? Briefly explain.
11. Give thought to the oft-heard term *the Trump effect*. To what extent has this "contention" impacted public school education during President Trump's tenure in the office of president to date?
12. Teacher retention reportedly is increasing to the extent that approximately 25 percent of the teacher personnel leave education after only one year in the classroom. Various reasons for this loss of talent could be listed. However, in your opinion, to what extent is teacher turnover due to the politics of education?

Case 4.1   I Tried to Tell Them, But They Just Wouldn't Listen

Homer Johnson had just been elected for a three-year term on the Lafayette School Board. Reportedly, his candidacy expenditures were double that of the other person who was contesting for the school board position. Johnson's TV ads and yard posters were viewed as being eye-catching. His campaign slogan, "Let's reimagine education for Lafayette students," did seem to catch the eye of the voters in a positive way.

Superintendent Martinez, other members of the school district's administrative staff, and local news media representatives, teacher representatives and several parents were in attendance at the first 2:00 p.m. meeting of the school board. The board meeting was opened by having each board member briefly review their background and basic interests in the goals of public education. New board member Johnson was first to speak. Johnson indicated that his primary career centered on business as related to investments. He commented that the contemporary slogan of "Make American, Buy American" was his belief as well.

"I decided to run for the school board position in order to gain a reimagining of our school district's curriculum," stated Johnson. "We need to reimagine our work forces in several respects. In view of the fact that our schools are no longer teaching our students how to do cursive writing or correctly using the King's English, why are we teaching the foreign languages of Spanish and German and now someone is recommending that we offer Chinese. If we agree to the slogan of 'Make American, Buy

American' then our education program should be teaching English and speaking English."

School board president, Dr. Roberta Martinez, thanked Mr. Johnson and was preparing to move on to the first next item on the board's agenda.

School superintendent, Daniel Serow, sat quietly in his chair at the table of the school board. His first thoughts centered on whether or not he should raise his hand and ask to speak at this point and time.

Discussion of Case Study 4.1

1. Assume the position of school superintendent Martinez. Think carefully about what you would do at this point and time. Under the circumstances, would you just sit and let Johnson's comments go by, or would you ask for the floor and respond in some manner to Johnson's comments? Keep in mind that the news media is present at the meeting and a board report is likely to be given during the 6:00 p.m. news.
2. Or, would you just wait until you are introduced at the board meeting for the superintendent's report? If so, what would you most likely include in your remarks? Would a response to board member Johnson's remarks be in order? Why or why not?
3. Think about the implications of Johnson's opening remarks at his first board meeting; both politically and administratively. How does Superintendent Martinez's political savvy come into play?

REFERENCES

Berkowitz, B., & Schulz, J. (2017). Involving key influentials in the initiative. *Community Tool Box*. Chapter 7, Section 6. Lawrence, KS: University of Kansas.

Bombeck, W. (1974). *Group vs. individual decision-making,* An unpublished doctoral dissertation, ASU, Department of Educational Administration and Policy Studies, Arizona State University, Tempe, Arizona.

Bottoms, G., & O'Neill, K. C. (2001). *Preparing a new breed of school principal; It's time for action.* Atlanta, GA: Southern Regional Educational Board (SREB).

Brown, A. (2011, April 14). Why schools need citizenship. *The Guardian*. Teaching Motorboard blog. London, United Kingdom.

Davies, D. R., and Brickell, H. M. (1988). *An instructional handbook on how to develop school board policies, by-laws, and administrative regulations.* Naco, AZ: Daniel R. Davies.

DaVinci Institute (2007, March 3). *Don't get blindsided by the future.* Futurist Speaker, Thomas Frey. Westminster, CO: author.

Grady, M. L., & Bryant, M. T. (1991, February). School board turmoil and superintendent turnover: What pushes them to the brink? *School Administration, 48*, (2). Alexandria, VA: AASA.

Hattie, John (2015). *What doesn't work in education: The politics of distraction.* London: Pearson.

Jacobsen, R. (2017, Spring). *EAD 943: Politics and education.* East Lansing, MI: Michigan State University.

Karns, A. (1970, October). *Politics: A vital force in education.* Alexandria, VA: Association for Supervision and Curriculum.

Morgan, G. (1986). *Images of organization.* First edition, Newbury Park, CA: Sage.

National Association of School Boards (1991). *Rules and relationships of school boards and superintendents.* Alexandria, VA: Authors.

Norton, M. S. (2015). *Teachers with the magic: Great teachers change students' lives.* Lanham, MD: Rowman & Littlefield.

Norton, M. S. (2017). *A guide for educational policy governance: Effective leadership for policy development.* Lanham, MD: Rowman & Littlefield.

Pashler, H., McDaniel, M., Rohrer, D., & Bjork, R. (2008). Learning styles: Concepts and evidence. *Psychological Science in the Public Interest,* 9 (3), 105–119. American Association of Psychological Science.

Shelton, B. S., et al. (1989). Perceived political factors related to superintendents' administration of school districts. *Education Research Journal,* 13 (2), 11–17.

Truty, J. (2006). *Politics savvy and labor.* HRD 313. Elusive and Vital. Paper presented at Midwest Research-to-Practice Conference in Adult/Continuing, and Community Education. St. Louis, MO: University of Missouri.

Turner, H. E. (1970). *Political power: Mobilizing political power for action.* Alexandria, VA: Association for Curriculum Development and Supervision.

Vicher, M. (2007). Teaching political savvy as a workforce skill. *Online Journal for Workforce Ed Development,* 2(3), 1–23. From the web: https://opensiuc.lib.siu.edu/ojwed/vol2/iss3/5/.

Wikipedia (2018, January 9). *Education; The future of education.* From the web: https://en.wikipedia,org/w/index.php?title=Educational&oldid=819384489

Winch, C., & Gingell, J. (2008). *Philosophy of education: The key concepts.* London & New York: Routledge, pp. 10–11.

Glossary

Action Research:
Research activities to solve an immediate problem led by an individual teacher or group of teachers.

Administrative Regulation:
Is related to a specific policy area of the school and is a precise statement that answers the question of "how to do."

Affective Characteristics:
Personal characteristics such as empathy, friendliness, positive attitude, and others that reveal a caring individual.

Alternative Education:
A broad concept that includes methods from self-directed and other forms of open learning.

Assister Analysis:
Serves to suggest ways to minimize resistance and learn to reason why objections are occurring.

Autodidact:
A person doing self-learning.

Autodidacticism:
Describes self-directed learning.

By-law:
A rule that relates to how the school board will govern itself.

Civics:
A study of the rights and responsibilities associated with becoming and/ or being a citizen of the United States. What it means to be a citizen of the United States.

Codification of Policies and Administrative Regulations:
A classification system for coding school policies and regulations commonly based on numbers or alpha letters.

Cognitive Characteristics:
Personal characteristics that center on information processing, conceptual resources, perceptual skills, language learning, or other aspects of brain development.

Collective Power:
The ability of a group to achieve its goals and objectives.

Common Core:
Mandated standards for program offerings and methods of instruction for public school curriculum set forth by the federal government.

Community Power Structure:
Is commonly viewed as being elite, factional, pluralistic, or inert.

Competitive Elite Power Structure:
Leadership is in different projects. It is more open, but groups often are vying for power. School board elections are hotly contested.

Compliance:
Workers do comply with the orders set forth by the authority but tend to disagree with them.

Creation Stage:
Commonly refers to the process of developing creative ability through exploration and expression.

Cross-disciplined Learning:
Learning that relates to or represents more than one branch of knowledge.

Cross-disciplined Power:
Relating to or representing more than one branch of knowledge; interdisciplinary.

Decision Engineering:
More recently called decision intelligence, it is a framework that unifies a number of best practices for organizational decision-making.

Distributive Power:
Refers to the physical distribution at intermediate points throughout the different power groups.

Division of Labor:
Specifically relates to the policy responsibilities of the local school board and the administrative regulation responsibilities of the school superintendent and professional staff.

Downward Power:
Is the authority that top officials in the organization hold to control the decision-making process.

Elite Monolithic Power Structure:
Is viewed as being closed and dominated by the prevailing political party. Receives little opposition in controlling the decision-making process.

Elite Power Structures:
The individuals or groups within the school community that have absolute power to decide what will or will not be decided on a policy issue or program approval; commonly represent a small percentage of the community population and often work behind the scenes.

Events Analysis:
The process of identifying the community powers by examining the persons closely involved and influential in approving the primary issues/ policies approved within the school community.

Factional Power Structures:
The individuals or groups of individuals who influence the making of processes in an organization that possess different opinions relative to issues and policy matters that are contended within the community.

Formal Education or Learning:
Learning that takes place in the traditional classroom with teachers in front of a class of students. The teacher teaches and the students are to learn.

Generation Z:
The generation that follows Generation Y; the Millennials.

Ideation Stage:
Creative process of generating, developing, and communicating new ideas where a new idea is understood as a basic element of thought.

Identification:
Workers tend to agree with the authority and carry out orders to the fullest degree.

Indigenous Learning:
Learning that is focused on regaining the cultures, languages, and values of a community.

Inert Power:
Power is placed in a more reserved capacity leaving the school superintendent to assume the leadership for recommending policies that the school board readily approves.

Influentials:
Persons who are knowledgeable of the community and can bring great influence to the decision-making process on school-community policies of importance.

Informal Learning:
Learning that takes place in a variety of settings whereby active learning can take place.

Inner Circles:
Commonly used to describe various school-community groups that are influential in various community matters. Most often are small closed groups consisting of business, industrial, government, and other such wealthy individuals.

Internalization:
If identification (see definition) is continued, internalization takes place on the part of the worker(s) if the orders are in agreement with their personal beliefs.

Knowledge Management:
A way in which organizational leaders take special means for keeping abreast of developing, sharing, and effectively using organizational knowledge; using the best of knowledge that exists in the organization.

Latent Power:
Power that is used to describe something that is capable of becoming active although it might not do so. The terms *quiescent power* and *static power* are also defined in this manner.

Legitimate Power:
See **position power**.

Local Control:
The belief that the local decisions about education should be made by persons within the local school community as opposed to the state or federal governance agencies.

Macropolitics:
Refers to how power is used at the various levels of government: local, state, and federal levels of government. Macro means large and commonly refers to nation and world politics.

Micro-credentialing:
The process of earning a mini-credential that is like a mini-degree or certification in a specific topic area.

Micropolitics:
Refers to how power is used in smaller governmental agencies such as a city or town or within a school or school system.

Millennials:
Persons reaching young adulthood around the year 2000. A generation also known as Generation Y; members want freedom to think and act creatively as individuals and teams.

Mission Statement:
A statement developed by school personnel that specifies the immediate goals and objectives.

Online Modules:
Modules that are designed to help teachers build or refresh their understanding of three important elements of learning—language, memory, and attention.

Open Education:
Education that is carried out by modern electronic technology.

Organizational Communication:
Refers to the channels of communication among and between members of the organization. It refers not only to how communication is channeled but to the quality of openness that exists in relation to availability and processes. A closed system commonly is one in which system members are viewed as talking primarily to themselves.

Participative Management:
The process of empowering members of a group, such as school employees, or citizens of a school community.

PERT:
A project management tool that requires two or more tasks forces to work with related program groups to coordinate tasks according to time targets that culminate in an ongoing evaluation and review of program goals.

Phenomenon-Based Learning:
The practice of having many different ways for student learning.

Pluralistic Power Structure:
Sometimes referred to as multiple-group power structure. Different individuals or groups assume the leadership depending on the issue at

hand. Each issue is discussed. In the end, voting is commonly unanimous. Democratic principles are followed.

Political Savvy:
The ability to understand and use the dynamics of power, organization, and decision-making to achieve objectives.

Politics of Distraction:
Those educational "innovations" that are emphasized as solutions for school improvement but tend to make little or no difference in student learning. These so-called solutions tend to be politically attractive but have little or no effect on student learning.

Politics of Education:
The ways in which governance institutions, political policy ideologies, and competing interests both within and without the education community influence the content, form, and functioning of schooling.

Position Power:
The power that accompanies an assigned role in the organization such as the CEO, bank manager, or school superintendent.

Power:
The ability to control the results of an issue or policy by means of getting it approved or being able to withhold it from consideration.

Power of Charisma:
The power derived from an individual's personal style or personal character traits. Also termed referent power.

Power of Information:
That quality possessed by an individual commonly called upon for the resolution of a problem facing the organization or group of people.

Power of Knowledge:
The ability to provide information that leads to the resolution of issues and problems facing the school.

Power of Knowledge or Expertise:
The ability to influence the decision-making process and provide valid answers for perplexing encounters and organizational issues.

Power of Punishment:
Is also referred to as coercive power and is vested in the ability to set forth sanctions that negatively impact on the unacceptable performance behavior of other individuals.

Power of Relationships:
The positive power gained through the outcome of positive relationships within a network of friends, colleagues, and acquaintances within or outside the organization.

Power of Rewards:
Is found in the ability to reward others for distinguished services and/or meeting other high standards.

Power Structure Analysis:
The procedure utilized to gain an understanding of how individuals go about expressing their power and to find out what issues, problems, and situations are those in which their power is utilized.

Progressive Era:
An historical era whereby the focus was on learning by doing. Education for social responsibility and lifelong learning were among the evident concepts of the time.

Register Analysis:
Refers to the degrees of formality with which populations use languages. The formal variables are also called codes.

Reputational Approach:
The process of going to persons in the school-community life and asking them to submit names of community influentials.

Resister Analysis:
Focuses on determining the reasons why the proposed change is being challenged.

Rule:
A requirement commonly set forth within a school or organization that sets forth what is required or prohibited relative to a matter such as behavior or procedure.

School Board Policy:
A general statement that sets forth the purposes, aims, and ends of what the school board wishes to accomplish in the education program.

Segmented Pluralism:
Is most open. Power acts depend on the issue at hand. School superintendent serves as a professional advisor. Issues are widely discussed.

Self-Directed Learning:
Learning that is realized by activities of the learner and accomplished by him or her.

Site-Based Management:
A governance form designed to shift the balance of authority among schools, districts, and the state. A school district might have site-based councils in every local school in the district that commonly include parents, teachers, students, administrators, and other citizens as members.

Social Network:
Uses network and graphic theories to investigate social structures within the school community.

Soldiering:
The practice of going through the motions of loyalty and high performance but only marching in place.

Team-Based Learning:
An instructional strategy that engages students by active learning and critical thinking. Students work in collaborative teams.

Technological Platforms:
A group of technological platforms that are used as a base upon which other applications or technologies are developed.

Upward Power:
Power influences vested in the subordinates of the organization.

Value Network:
A business analysis that describes special and technical resources within the school community.

Virtual Power:
Educationally, power that is a process of integrating several sources of power so as to improve the overall power results for the organization.

Virtual Teams:
Teams of individuals who work together from different locations, geographically. Commuting is accomplished electronically. Provides an opportunity to use the best talents from all locations.

About the Author

Dr. **M. Scott Norton** has served as a secondary school teacher of mathematics, coordinator of curriculum for the Lincoln, Nebraska School District, assistant superintendent for instruction, and superintendent of schools in Salina, Kansas, before joining the University of Nebraska as professor and vice chair of the Department of Educational Administration and Supervision. Later he served as professor and chair of the Department of Educational Administration and Policy Studies at Arizona State University, where he is currently professor emeritus.

His primary graduate research and instruction areas include curriculum and supervision, teaching methods, governance policy, instructional leadership, educational leadership, human resources administration, the assistant school principalship, research methods, organizational development, and competency-based administration.

He has published widely in national journals in such areas as teaching/instructional methods, curriculum development, organizational climate, instructional leadership, gifted student programs, student retention, and others.

Most recent textbooks authored by Dr. Norton include:

1. *Dealing with Change: The Effects of Organizational Development on Contemporary Practices* (2018). Rowman & Littlefield, London, New York, Lanham, MD.
2. *Guiding Curriculum Development: The Need to Return to the Local Level* (2016). Rowman & Littlefield.
3. *Teachers with the Magic: Great Teachers Change Students' Lives* (2015). Rowman & Littlefield.

4. *The Principal as a Learning Leader: Motivating Students by Emphasizing Achievement* (2013). Rowman & Littlefield.
5. *The Principal as a Student Advocate: A Guide for Doing What's Best for All Students* (2012). Norton, Kelly & Battle, Eye on Education, Larchmont, NY.
6. *A Guide for Educational Policy Development: Effective Leadership for Policy Development* (2017). Rowman & Littlefield.
7. *Guiding the Human Resources Function: New Issues, New Needs* (2017). Rowman & Littlefield.
8. *The Principal as Human Resources Leader: A Guide to Exemplary Practices for Personnel Administration* (2015). Routledge, London, New York.
9. *The Legal World of the School Principal: What Leaders Need to Know about School Law* (2016). Rowman & Littlefield.
10. *The Changing Landscape of School Leadership: Recalibrating the School Principalship* (2015). Rowman & Littlefield.
11. *The Whitehouse and Education through the Years: Presidents' Educational Views and Significant Educational Contributions* (2018). Rowman & Littlefield, Lanham, MD.

Dr. Norton has received several state and national awards honoring his services and contributions to the field of educational administration from such organizations as the American Association of School Administrators, the University Council for Educational Administration, the Arizona Administrators Association, the Arizona Educational Research Association, Arizona State University College of Education Dean's Award for excellence in service to the field, president of the ASU College of Education Faculty Association, and the distinguished service award from the Arizona Information Service. He presently is serving as a member of the ASU Emeritus College Council.

Dr. Norton's state and national leadership positions have included service as executive director of the Nebraska Association of School Administrators, a member of the board of directors for the Nebraska Congress of Parents and Teachers, president of the Nebraska Council of Teachers of Mathematics, president of the Arizona School Administrators Higher Education Division, member of the Arizona School Administrators Board of Directors, staff associate of the University Council for Educational Administrators, treasurer of the University Council for School Administrators, Nebraska State Representative for the National Association of Secondary School Principals, member of the board of editors for the American Association of School Public Relations, and presently a governance council member for the Emeritus College of Arizona State University.